KI[illegible] R'S

or

The Ballad of Sir Softpaws

by
Rhys Reed-Johnson

'S CAT

me parts by Robin Price.

www.mogzilla.co.uk

Printed in the UK

AUTHOR'S DEDICATION

To George Canning (R.Hon), the Dallas Cowboys, and the guy who invented the cheeseburger.

Though we will never meet, I know you'd buy this book at market price. Apologies to Sir Thomas Malory and many Welshmen.

Chapter I
A Right Royal Ruckus

King Arthur crept into his bedroom for a well-deserved beauty sleep. The hour was late and he'd spent a long day judging the Roundtable Talent Show. Sir Percival had got the rabbit stuck in his top hat. Sir Galahad almost did the splits and Sir Gawain's poetry almost rhymed. Being king was tiring, Arthur thought, as he climbed into his four-poster bed. No doubt something worse would come along tomorrow.

Soon Arthur was sound asleep and snoring loudly, dreaming of great deeds done by brave heroes. In his dreams, Arthur replaced these heroes with images of himself doing all their great deeds instead. Also his horse was made of candyfloss. Sleep was fun! But all around Camelot, not a sound was to be heard except the hoot of a short-sighted owl and the thud it made when it accidentally flew into the castle wall.

All of a sudden there was a loud bang, then a kapow, three more bangs, a pop, and some very naughty words only known to certain wizards. Arthur woke with a jolt but remained firmly beneath his sheets. Many strange noises were heard in Camelot, especially at night. From the marching band of magic potatoes to all-peasant pig parties, it was truly the castle that never slept. Not everything needed Arthur's attention and his royal sorting out of problems. That was until there came the loudest bang anyone had ever heard, even louder than the time a local dragon tried to learn the drums.

With that bang, Arthur ordered his minstrels to stop playing his 'whale sounds' sleepy-time music and gave a big, fed-up yawn. He took off his sleeping mask, fumbled for his dressing gown, and waved his feet around until they found his fluffy slippers. Then he leapt out of bed with a kingly grumble to explore the cause of what was making all that banging.

But what was making all that banging sounded big and dangerous, so Arthur grabbed his famous sword, Excalibur, for safety. Unfortunately, in the darkness, the king's hand found the sharp end of the legendary sword (that happened more than he would have liked). With an "ow", the blade fell from his royal fingers and left even deeper scuff marks on the royal oak floorboards.

"What is all that racket?" mumbled Guinevere from her side of the bed. "I thought we got rid of the drumming dragon."

"When I find out, it's going to get an almighty poke from Excalibur," replied Arthur. "Nobody interrupts the king's special snoozy time. Me and Teddy were fighting sand giants and I was about to be crowned king of Gumball Island."

"Of course you were," mumbled Guinevere. She instantly fell back to sleep.

So then, Arthur opened a door and charged without fear into his shoe closet. Guinevere sighed heavily, got out of bed, and pushed Arthur in the direction of the hallway.

"Thank you, Gwinny," whispered the king. "Now to search the rest of the castle." He was answered with a bedroom door slammed in his face.

With nothing but candlelight guiding his path, the king tiptoed quietly through the hallway ignoring the bangs, booms and kapows that lay further ahead. The racket was coming from the tower on the far side of the castle. Merlin's laboratory was there. The shifty wizard was known to sneak around after dark. He did his best work around bedtime when he was less likely to be arrested. In the past, Arthur had put up with Merlin's "side projects". There was the all-male giraffe brass band, the underground theme park, "Scream in a can", the bagpipe black market. One time, he invented indoor golf with dynamite instead of golf balls. But even Merlin knew to keep the noise down after seven. This time he had gone too far. Whatever was going on, Arthur would get to the bottom of it using what little mercy a children's book will allow.

"When I get my hands on that wizard..." thought Arthur before he went scaredy-cat. "But, hang on a minute. What if it's a robber pretending to be Merlin? He might want to steal my sword." Just then, there was another loud bang.

"Oh no, a robber," thought Arthur again. "For sure, it must be a robber. I'd better hide."

And hid the cowardly king did. Behind an empty suit of armour, Arthur could hear footsteps coming down the hall. They were getting closer. Closer to him. With a big swing, Arthur closed his eyes and waved Excalibur at the target.

"Ah ha! Got you, robber!" squeaked Arthur, in a higher pitched voice than he was aiming for.

"G-g-g-g good swing, my liege," stammered Sir Galahad in his pyjamas. "You were v-very close to hitting me."

The king had stuck his sword into a priceless antique table, missing Galahad's head by inches.

"Sorry Galahad, I thought you were a robber!" said Arthur, patting the old knight on the head. Galahad fainted.

Chapter 2
Merlin's Massive Mishap

Arthur tried to hide his mistake. He stuffed Galahad's body behind a nearby curtain but by now a small crowd had gathered. There were many round table knights, cleaners, Guinevere herself, and a tourist who was dropping by. They all stood and stared at the king in amazement.

"Well done, my lord! You have defeated the sleepwalking Sir Galahad," said Sir Lancelot. As a loyal knight of Camelot, he tried to start a cheer and save the king's blushes.

"A mighty foe," Arthur chimed in. "And while I was still wearing my slippers."

Lancelot sighed. He had seen Arthur do much worse with many more eyes watching.

"But now is not the time to practice sword fighting," said Lancelot. "There's a loud banging coming from Merlin's tower. Bad magic, I bet."

"I might have known," growled Arthur, still pulling at his stuck sword.

"That wizard really sometimes takes the biscuit," added Guinevere, checking on Galahad. He would need warm milk tonight. An extra teddy bear too.

"Without a strong king keeping him in line, Merlin will be the end of us all!" Arthur groaned. He finally yanked out his sword and split the table in two.

"And the end of my furniture!" Guinevere shot Arthur an evil look.

Arthur ignored it. Pointing Excalibur towards the tower, it was time to talk to Merlin.

When the party had reached the tower, four brave knights pushed open the doors to Merlin's room, ignoring the signs that read "No entrie!" and "Abandone hope, all you who enter hear!" Merlin had painted these himself. Unfortunately there was no magic that could improve his spelling. With the doors forced open, they all entered. The room was dark. In the shadows, there was very little you could be sure you had seen. Arthur fumbled around feeling ticked off. He was on the lookout for quick answers and an excuse to return to bed.

"Merlin!" boomed the king, "If you're building exploding cushions again, I'll make you eat one!" At last, Guinevere lit a small candle. It gave off a dim glow and shone a little light on Merlin's laboratory. Everything was dusty or busted or crusty or rusted and there was the usual bad smell. There were many unused spells. There were many unfinished inventions. There were many half-eaten sandwiches. Merlin never did anything right, but the old wizard was nowhere to be seen.

"Oh! If he's left Camelot without paying his bills, I will be one mean queen," said Guinevere. She clenched her fists with fury. Merlin always pretended to be under a 'memory loss' spell every time the queen brought up his debts (it was the one thing he never forgot to do). Just then, a breeze blew through the window and snuffed out her candle. Everything was dark once again.

"Bother!" Arthur thought. He fumbled about for a light but only stubbed his toes. Surrounded by nothing but black, all the king could see were two green eyes the size of footballs gazing back at him. They took a step toward him with furry paws the size of grand pianos. Then came a row of sharp smiling teeth from a mouth big enough to swallow him like an after dinner mint. Its breath smelt of fish and it seemed hungry.

"Guinevere, is that you?" asked Arthur. He patted the thing on its wet nose.

"Roar!" roared a booming voice.

"Excuse me, my mistake." Arthur calmly cleared his throat and stretched. He wanted to make sure his screams didn't strain his throat when he ran away.

"Aaaaaaaaaaarrrrrrrgggggggggghhhhhhh!" screamed the king. "Run for your lives! Women and Kings first!"

Arthur dashed out of the room as fast as his cowardly feet could carry him, shoving his slower friends out the way. With the king leading the way, there was a mad rush for the exit with much pushing and tripping. Where this giant scary mystery came from and what it wanted, nobody knew. Nobody wanted to stick around and find out. Soon, everyone had escaped into the hallway. While the others tried to catch their breath, Arthur slammed the door shut with a mighty crash. He looked around for a hammer, some nails, and a few great big pieces of heavy wood. As usual, there were never any when he needed them.

"How's Merlin?" asked Lancelot, picking at his fingernails. He hadn't been paying attention. For him, danger was a daily event.

"There's something in there, Sir Spots-not-a-lot. Something big. Something very big. Something very big that strangely smells of fish. But it's not Merlin!" snapped the angry king. "Now fetch me some big pieces of heavy wood and let's never speak of it again."

"So... no Merlin. Shame. We were going to play tennis this Saturday. Do you know any good doubles partners in Camelot?" Nothing seemed to scare Lancelot as he practiced his backhand.

Arthur's servants dabbed his sweaty brow with a swooning cloth, (damsel strength).

"Whatever is in there wants a late night snack and I don't mean milk and cookies," said the king, double-checking that Merlin's door was shut. "Only an idiot would go back in there with such a scary monster stomping about," he added.

"Or a true and noble knight," replied Lancelot, flexing his muscles.

"Same thing," sighed Arthur. He wasn't wrong.

An almighty roar blew the doors clean off their hinges. Now, there was a terrible stink of fish coming from Merlin's laboratory drifting into the hallway. A deep voice growled, waiting in the darkness. The creature was in no rush. Any time was good to pick off Arthur and his knights one by one like a box of chocolates.

Arthur looked at the knights. "Any volunteers?"

The knights looked at the floor. After a few minutes of nudging each other, no one came forward. All agreed it was best to stand bravely aside and let somebody else go first.

Guinevere sighed at these chickens in chainmail. Taking the crown from her head, she casually lobbed it through the door into the darkness. Sweetly, she said, "Oh no, I've lost my crown. Sounds like a hero's quest if ever I heard one. Won't somebody fetch it for me?"

"Nope!" chorused the knights.

"What do you mean nope?" snapped the queen, not so sweetly. "Why do we even have knights if they can't gang up and beat a simple monster?"

"After you," said Arthur, leading by example.

"No, after you!" said Sir Lancelot, pushing forward Sir Gawain.

"No, no, after you!" said Sir Gawain, elbowing Sir Boris.

"No, no, no, after you," said Sir Boris. He pushed the king forward.

"No, no, I'm the king, you all have to do what I say!" growled Arthur.

"Safety first, especially mine," said a knight.

"Mine too," said another knight.

"I hear crowns are pretty cheap these days," added yet another knight.

"Maybe she has a spare," suggested a fourth knight.

"I just want a good night's sleep," said a knight with comic timing.

The knights laughed at the joke. They all enjoyed a good pun.

"It'll be alright on the night," said another knight waiting for the laugh.

But the knights didn't laugh. One pun was enough.

"What were we talking about?" asked the last knight.

And that, dear bored reader, was the last of the knight jokes, I promise.

After a few quick games of 'sword – parchment – boulder', it was decided Sir Gawain would enter first (parchment covers boulder, of course). He would have the honour of defeating the monster or becoming a tasty treat. Both options were fine by Arthur. As Gawain entered the laboratory with knocking knees and legs like jelly, the king and his luckier knights hid behind the curtains.

"Here monster, monster, monster," whimpered Sir Gawain. "Here monster, monster, monster!"

"Louder and braver!" yelled a voice from the curtain.

At that, Gawain searched the laboratory high and low in total silence. Among the shadows, he hoped he wouldn't find anything. He also hoped "anything" wouldn't find him either. For a while, except for bumping into tables and knocking over some glass flasks, his wish was granted. When there was no sound of bones being crunched or a gigantic beasty burp, the curtain asked "Well, did you find the monster?"

There was no reply, not even a manly scream.

"Gawain? Don't make me go in there!" said Arthur, eyeing his next victim behind the curtain (Sir Tristan).

"I'm fine, sire," Gawain said. He searched some more but still no monster was found. "Hello, is anyone there?" he asked.

"Of course something's in there, you nit!" roared Arthur, shaking in rage. "You're supposed to find out what it is!"

"Ummm," stumbled the knight. "I can't see anything. It's too dark."

"Use the candle" snorted Arthur. There was a small pause as they waited.

"Not working, sire," replied Gawain.

"Light it!" snapped the king.

"I don't want to," said the knight. "He might see me."

"But he can still hear you," said Arthur. And that was the final word on that.

Gawain thought for a second and tried to light the candle without being seen. He ignored the heavy whump that leapt off Merlin's bookcase and landed close behind him.

"What if it went away on its own?" the knight hoped. "Does that mean I can go back to bed?"

At that, the king threw one of his shoes, missing him by a good metre and hitting the monster behind Gawain square on the head.

"Meow!" roared the beast with a sore head.

"Meow?" echoed a confused Gawain.

"Meow!" confirmed the beast, swatting Gawain back into the corridor with a clangy thump. The impact knocked down the curtain, ruining Arthur's favourite hiding place.

As the knights hid behind one another like a scaredy pants conga line, an enormous furry paw padded into view, then another. Out came pointed ears bigger than a shed's roof. Followed by whiskers the size of snooker cues. Then there was a long stretch of bright orange fur longer than a school bus. Finally there was a scaly dragon's tail that felt totally out of place. It shook side to side, putting a hole through the castle walls. As the creature emerged fully into the light, King Arthur immediately recognised him. It was the royal cat. His pet.

"Sir Softpaws! Is that you?" Arthur asked.

"Meow!" replied Sir Softpaws. He meant "Yes!"

"Sir Softpaws! My kitty cat kittykins! What have they done to you?" cried the king, throwing his arms around a furry leg thicker than an oak tree. He was greeted with a warm lick that felt like being slapped by a soaking wet pillow case.

"Meow!" said Sir Softpaws like most normal cats. It wasn't much of an explanation, but Sir Softpaws was a very normal cat. At least that was true before Merlin's mischief had made him a scary giant. Usually, he was about half the height of Arthur's knees (which had stopped knocking in fear). Now his head scraped the ceiling. His once high pitched mew was now so low and thundering that it shook the tower to its very foundations.

"Well, it appears the mystery of the midnight monster has been solved," said Lancelot. "Looks like his highness was overfeeding his cat again." He yawned, stretched, and patted his tummy. "Time for this tired knight to get some shut eye."

"Here! Here!" agreed the rest and they headed back to the magical land of Beddington-Under-Sheets.

But King Arthur was hopping mad at what strangeness had happened to his cat.

"You wait right here!" he commanded. "I feed Sir Softpaws the right amount of food for a cat his size."

A knight raised a hand to ask a question.

"I mean a cat the size he used to be!" Arthur had no time for malarky. "By royal decree, this mystery is not over, not while a member of the royal family is in distress." He pointed at Sir Softpaws who had sat himself down and began to groom himself. "Look at him! That cat's a blubbering mess. Oh when I find Merlin, he'll be cleaning the castle toilets from now until Christmas!" growled the king. If Arthur ever calmed down, he might lend him a brush. "We'll search the entire castle if we have to."

All at once, the knights groaned. Search they did, and they spent the rest of bedtime looking around the entire castle for Merlin. But there was no sign of him anywhere. They reported back to Arthur who was reading a book of the wizard's titled: Revenge Magic: Extra Painful Edition. He was halfway through the chapter on sharks.

Sir Percival stepped forward. "My king, Merlin's disappeared like, like…"

"Don't you dare say it…" pleaded Arthur, smelling the joke a mile away.

"Like magic!" one knight chuckled.

Arthur screamed and threw his remaining shoe. It broke a window.

"Sorry my lord, but he really has. There's no trace of the cheating stinkpot anywhere. We searched the dungeons. We searched the roof. We spent hours going through the king's private games room. We spent even more time in the royal toy chest. We looked everywhere for him and came up one wizard short. You could say Merlin has gone Merl...out!".

The knights fell about laughing once again. Before they could make any more annoying jokes of this sort, Arthur cut them off with a swift jab to the bottom from Excalibur. The knights backed away. The famous sword was a popular means of keeping knights in order with its promise of a well-deserved poking.

"Find Merlin this instant!" ordered Arthur. "I can't have a giant cat and a missing wizard. What will the other kingdoms think?" Having said these words, the king fell over into a deep snooze.

Chapter 3
The Quest to Make Sir Softpaws Normal Again

Days went by but still Merlin did not return. When something went wrong like this, the wizard would typically go into hiding and lie low until the fuss had died down. Arthur had double-checked Merlin's usual hiding places: the cake section of the castle pantry; the queen's trampoline; the Camelot archery park and soft play area. Sadly, there was no sign of the sneaky sorcerer.

By now, all of Camelot had heard about Sir Softpaws and his monstrous size. The oversized kitten was too big to be kept indoors so Arthur decided to let him roam around the kingdom, hoping his peasants could share in his misery. Wherever Softpaws went, giant paw prints were left behind where people's houses used to be. He ate markets out of business. He sank all the fishing boats. He even drank the moat dry. When he chased butterflies, he was like a runaway steamroller. Being such a cat of destruction, the Softpaws name no longer suited him.

Nevertheless, the cat was a smash hit with the locals, even if there wasn't a single roof in the kingdom that hadn't been flattened. Far from fearing Softpaws, Camelot had adopted him as their town mascot. You could walk for miles but you wouldn't find anyone who said a bad word against the fluffy destroyer with the wet nose.

"Only in Camelot!" laughed a grey bearded farmer as Sir Softpaws batted his cart around like a ball of string. "Too bad he scared away my horses. Oh well, I forgive him."

"I tell you we must have the biggest cat in Britain," said a mother of five. "Before then we only had the biggest twit wearing a crown."

"What do you think about that? King Fredrick of Frankia?" added Rudolph Shortsword. A part-time blacksmith and dance teacher who was easily riled up about rival kingdoms.

"That lovely kitty-cat will make me even richer yet!" said Terry Cotter, the richest man in Camelot. He had a talent for making money out of a crisis. Of course, with Arthur on the throne, every day was pay day. "I'm now selling roofs that smell like dog food." It was a smart plan. One whiff and Softpaws had belched up a hairball that briefly blotted out the sun. "Who wants to see Britain's biggest hairball? One gold farthing per gander."

"Hooray! Hurrah!" shouted the sort of people who shout things out spontaneously. And in a split second, Terry Cotter was even richer.

Everyone cheered wherever the massive moggie went, making King Arthur very jealous.

Back in the castle, this latest Softpaws gossip was as well received as a pair of garlic socks.

"I don't get it. Why would Merlin want to make the cat big?" asked Guinevere sitting on her throne. She looked rather grey under her eyes. Softpaws had developed a deep meow which could be heard throughout the land. Plus, he had always been a night time cat. Sleep was difficult.

"I don't know," snapped Arthur as he walked back and forth. "I never know what goes on with that conjuring crackpot."

"And, unless I'm mistaken..." she added. "Does he have a dragon's tail?"

"Yes, and he can breathe fire," said Arthur in a low grumble.

"Fire?" Guinevere was shocked.

"He can now breathe fire." Arthur tugged at his singed hair to prove the point. "Isn't Merlin wonderful?" he added sarcastically. "A true hero of the kingdom."

"Oh dear!" said the queen. "Hmm, bad magic and no mistake."

Arthur gave a heavy sigh and walked to the window.

Outside, Sir Softpaws was mobbed by happy Camelotians who filled the courtyard. He burped out a fireball and set fire to the local school. All the children cheered and formed a ring around him, skipping with joy. The people loved him more and more.

"A true hero of the kingdom," the king repeated under his breath.

"Who knows? Maybe this time Merlin has his reasons," suggested the queen.

"When has Merlin ever had a good reason for doing anything?" said Arthur in a strop. "Remember when he turned every tree in the kingdom into sticks of candy floss? I spent an entire week saying sorry to angry villagers with toothache."

Guinevere nodded sympathetically. "All the dentists of Camelot erected a statue in his honour." The queen gave a silent chuckle, then pretended she didn't.

"Or there was the time he magicked my horse into a salmon, and I had to address the entire kingdom on fishback."

Guinevere nodded in sympathy. "Shame. That was one of your better speeches. Not funny whatsoever." She giggled. "Pardon me I, uh, coughed."

"Or what about the time he put itching powder in my shampoo and told everyone I'd invented a brand new dance?" added Arthur, scratching his scalp free of the bad memory.

Guinevere simply nodded. Feeling the king's pain, she slammed her hand hard on her thigh and spat out a booming laugh. The whole itching thing had been extremely funny. People called it the "Funky Arthur."

"Sorry Arthur, I…. ha, ha. I... ha, ha, ha," Guinevere collapsed into a fit of titters and began rolling along the floor. Arthur let out a scorned huff.

"If you're not going to take it seriously, it looks like I'll have to solve everything by myself." At that the king marched out the door, adding "Merlin's not the only one in the realm who knows a thing about magic."

Later that day, Arthur arrived at the royal stables. He called for the stableboys to saddle up his trusty steed so he might search all Britain for a way to shrink the gigantic cat. The king's horse still smelled terrible, thanks to Merlin's little experiment. His name had once been 'Swiftfoot' but because of his foul stink the stableboys nicknamed him 'Whiffywoo', or 'Whiffy' for short (he had his own stable far away from the other horses).

Arthur climbed onto Whiffy's back and prepared for his journey. He headed towards the Camelot market. When going on a long quest, it's important to be well stocked. The king had his sword sharpened and polished to a nice sheen. Next, he bought enough packed lunches to last until winter. Then he stacked up on barrels of oats and hay to keep Whiffy happy.

After that he bought a small book of 'fairy phrases', got the maps redrawn, and had his passport stamped. At last, Arthur was ready to leave.

He trotted through the streets toward the drawbridge. People waved the king "goodbye" and wished him luck but made sure to cover their noses because of the horse. In the distance, high above the houses, Arthur could see Sir Softpaws. He had flipped a bakery upside down and was helping himself to any spare cakes he found. The king stared at the cat and tried to put himself in the cat's shoes (or paws). "Soon, my kitty compadre," Arthur thought to himself. "Soon, you will be back to normal and we will play like we used to."

And so Arthur set out from Camelot on a quest. As far as quests go, I would rate it 'medium' on the strangeness scale – somewhere between slaying a dragon and marrying a different, prettier dragon. But like all quests, there were many miles on horseback before anything interesting happened.

Chapter 4
Something Interesting Happened

After taking a left at the Haunted Forest, past the Swamp of Doom, a hard right by the Club for Retired Trolls, and straight down Lady of the Lake Avenue, Arthur had reached a place he had not visited in many months.

It was a strange place far away from Camelot, the kind of spot where a king could run away after his latest whoopsie. Arthur knew it well. Usually, the angry mob gave up once he was past the row of talking trees. Fewer still tried to cross the river that 'guesses your weight' out loud. And anyone Arthur had really ticked off normally called it quits after being robbed by bridge trolls. This was one of his favourite hiding places: 'The Land of Majestic Magical Folk' (twinned with Spellchester-on-Sea).

Spending many days and nights galloping about for answers, Arthur sought out every magical user and every enchanted creature he could find (including maths teachers). Alas, nobody was any help, but the king did pick up a recipe for beetroot soup. Of course, there was a problem. All the serious spell casting folk were in league with each other and were very hostile to outsiders (the soup recipe had side effects like turning your feet into cheese). Also, magic folk are famously picky about what jobs they choose, especially if the spell had already been started by another wizard. Like chickens, witches and wizards have a firm pecking order.

Arthur stopped at a tavern called "The Duck and Gandalf". He tied Whiffy the horse to a nearby ice cream stand, causing the elf who was selling the treats to pass out from the smell. The king entered and saw the usual crowd. There were witches enjoying happy hour, teams of goblins in sunglasses, four werewolves playing 'I spy', shifty wizards selling weight loss potions, a band of knights searching for holy spoons, some sleeping dwarves and a dog with a crystal ball who could predict your fortunes but could only say 'woof'. In other words, the usual crowd.

“What’ll it be, scrub?” asked a half-man, half-horse behind the bar. His name badge read ‘Centaur Steve’.

“Two king colas and a bowl of cursed chips, please,” replied the king.

“Coming right up,” said Steve and trotted on his hooves to the kitchen. Behind the door, he could be heard arguing with the cook, who was a bag of onion rings magically brought to life.

Arthur sat himself down at a table littered with nibbled chicken bones and burger buns. He pulled out his list of enchanted folk he had already visited. He must have talked to every wizard, witch, warlock, wise woman, party magician, and card shark throughout the land. The king continued down the magical rankings until he reached disgraced wizards, discount witches, weekend warlocks, not terribly wise women, rabbits without top hats, and a man called Ploppy Poltergeist, a plumber who smelled worse than his horse. All were clueless in how to shrink an oversized cat. Arthur had crossed many names on the list. Then he gave a grumpy sigh and pondered in his head if he was really out of options, until Steve returned with his meal.

“Ya know,” began Steve, whose arm was covered in fresh onion ring burns (the cook had attacked him), “there’s one person who might be able to help you with your cat problem.” Arthur looked at him with hope as the centaur continued. “Doesn’t ask any questions. Not too expensive. Not found on any magic lists, neither. He’s almost a good bloke… almost.” Steve popped open two king colas and flung a bowl of cursed chips in front of Arthur. The chips screamed at the king (that’s how you knew they were fresh).

“But Sir Softpaws will still be able to walk and drink milk, right?” asked Arthur with a raised untrusting eyebrow. A few chips had made a run for it and escaped his grasp.

“Very well,” added Steve. “I know someone else who can help you with your cat problem.”

Steve produced a small map that doubled as a place mat. “If you go past the thingamabob there and avoid the vile whosit here, there’s this lake, ya see, the lake –”

“Pass,” said Arthur, sensing where this was going. “We’re not on speaking terms.”

“Oh, so you’ve met the famous Lady of the Lake.” Steve

was impressed.

"Once or twice," said Arthur, his eyes darted back and forth. "Twice was enough."

"Well, it looks like you're out of options friend. It's either make nice with the lake lady or you're up a creek without a paddle." Steve was right.

"But..." cringed Arthur, "she's so mean." By now, all his chips had fled.

"Yeah, she is!" continued Steve. "A right meaney on a bad day. Sometimes she comes into my tavern complaining about this stupid king in Camelot. Name's King 'Awful' or 'Halfwit' or something. She promises four free wishes to anyone who finds him and leaves him outside a dragon's lair covered in BBQ sauce." The centaur began to gallop in excitement. "Of course, you have to show her the burned crown afterwards."

"Umm. Well, good thing my name's not halfwit,' said Arthur, who was a quarterwit at best. He slowly got up from his chair and tiptoed toward the exit. "Well, time for me to hit the trail. Better late than never." Arthur reached for the door. "Nothing like the present and all that. Am I right?"

"But you didn't touch the fries!" Steve called out. "I can catch them if you like." The chips had fled down a mousehole and were making a 'mice/chips alliance' where they promised to always fight against humans. Their revenge would be never-ending.

"No, thank you. I had a singing cheeseburger for lunch. That'll see me through the day." And just like that, King Awful had bolted out the tavern and was galloping away down a dusty road before you could say cheese and potatoes.

Chapter 5
Puddles of Ill-Will

By the time Arthur reached the enchanted lake from his youth, he was very tired and his thirsty horse was looking forward to a nice, cool drink. Unfortunately, both rider and steed soon discovered the once deep and wide lake had strangely dried up. In the past, its waters stretched the length of a hundred elephants (trunk to trunk). Now what was left was little more than a small muddy puddle. Clearly, the lake had fallen on hard times. Whiffy was furious.

As the horse tried to suck water from some nearby clumps of grass, Arthur sat down on the mud and thought. He wondered what had happened and what to rename this once magical place (Bognor Regis came to mind. PlopTown came quickly after. The winner was Ploppy Regis).

Just then, a ghostly arm dramatically rose from out of the brown puddle. As wrist and elbow slowly climbed above the waters, they were joined by a soaking wet woman in a white dress now covered in nasty looking stains. She was beyond the help of soap. This was the famous Lady of what used to be a Lake.

The smell coming off her was so foul that it nearly blotted out the smell of Arthur's horse (nearly). Once this Lady had given the king his legendary sword, Excalibur. Now she looked like she wanted to give him a knuckle sandwich. Arthur waved at her like an idiot.

"Well, well, well. Look who had the nerve to show up?" yelled the sodden dame.

"Greetings, Puddle Lady," answered Arthur. "I–"

"That's still Lady of the Lake to you, halfwit!" snapped the pongy woman.

"You say 'potato' and I say 'portarto,'" replied the king. The Lady just looked puzzled. There was a short strained silence. "It's the same thing… I mean," said Arthur.

"No it's not, you nit! There's no such thing as a portarto! What nonsense you spout," she said in a chilly voice. "Now, leave my lake before you get a very smelly splashing!"

"OK, OK, Lady OF THE Lake. I'm sorry," Arthur said,

trying to make peace. He was never very good at making peace. "Sore point, but, what happened to your lake?"

It was a sore point, but a fair one too. She was squatting in a puddle no deeper than a trout on a diet. 'Whiffy' the horse was trying to drink what little water was left, but having no luck. The lady let out a heavy (and angry) grunt.

"Sometimes I wonder why I ever gave you that sword, you big goof! Why are you here?"

Arthur was taken by surprise. He had to come up with a face-saving lie on the spot.

"Well, um, I was er... chatting with Guinevere about this and that and things and thingamajigs, and we were thinking: who do we know who knows magic like the back of her hand? The best at magic, so to speak. The best bestest at magic, in fact. Your name came up right away. Couldn't think of anyone more perfect. So I was wondering if you might—"

"So, Merlin's made another mess, has he?" came the reply. The Lady of the Puddle was nobody's fool.

"Oh Damsel of the Damp, you know me so well," blushed the king. His poor attempt at charm fell flatter than a bungee-jumping pancake.

"Don't call me Damsel of the Damp! It's Lady of the Lake. Lake, I say!" ordered the angry woman. "You want to know what happened to my lake? Do you? Merlin happened!"

"Of course, he did." Arthur sighed and sat down again. Stories that had the word 'Merlin' in them were often upsetting and went on for ages.

The Lady began. "It was a few weeks ago. Your wiley wizard passed this way. He claimed he could clean my whole lake for as little as a silver penny. On my salary, I'd be a fool not to take him up on the offer. It was easy, he claimed. All I had to do was sign my name on the dotted line and treat myself to a short holiday."

Arthur nodded politely, seeing where this was going. Merlin's favourite weapon was the dotted line (on every contract). The Lady would not be his last. Right now, her story was only half done.

"So, hey presto, I came back home a few days later. Not only was my lake spotless, thanks to Merlin, but he had signed over all my water to the 'King Cola' company. Have you heard of the 'King Cola' company?"

Arthur shook his head. Thankfully the bottles he bought at the tavern were now gone. He had thrown them in a magic bush on the ride over. The king was a stinking litterbug.

"Over the next few weeks," the Lady continued. "They began to build. Soon dirty great metal pipes and gigantic vacuum cleaners were sucking up my lake and turning my water into a million bottles of cola. Now I'm almost homeless and Merlin's lawyers blame it on the hot weather! There's a water shortage apparently… according to the King Cola family."

Behind her, the Lady pointed to an evil looking factory that blotted out the sun, casting the magical forest in deep, dark shadow. It had been there the entire time, but the authors hadn't mentioned this fact earlier in case it upset our young readers. The black brickwork was particularly evil. The copper pipes were already rusted. The steam vents were causing a nearby rabbit to cough. On each of the smoke belching chimneys read the words 'King Cola'. One displayed a flashy drawing of a gigantic cartoon Merlin giving the 'thumbs up' to anyone who passed by. His speech bubble promised "Good times and Great taste" – endorsed by King Arthur (of Camelot). The reason for the lake's recent shrinkage was obvious.

Arthur's face turned the same bright red colour as King Cola's new cherry soda, and he tried to steer talk back to his kitty quest. On a rusty pipe, some factory workers were pointing and laughing at him and sharing a refreshing bottle of 'King Cola' on their lunch break. The king regretted how many bottles he'd drunk since leaving his kingdom but knew to keep his mouth shut – even though he couldn't deny the fantastic taste. They really were fun for any occasion.

Realizing the Lady probably didn't want to hear about their new pineapple and passion fruit summer special, Arthur tried to butter her up with promises.

"Lady of the Lake, I promise, if you can shrink my cat, I'll see Merlin banned from Camelot and forced to live under a bridge with the smelliest of trolls. And the King Cola people will join him. This I promise." But the Lady wouldn't budge.

"No can do, you scrubby land-dweller," said the Lady as she poked her tongue out at the factory workers. "My magic relies on water. It's a package deal. As you can see, no water equals no magic. Either we hope for many rainstorms, or we can wait until the King Cola company goes bankrupt."

"Well, now I am in quite a pickle," Arthur mused. "A very watery pickle. A gherkin. I am a gherkin. I am in a jar of gherkins," said the king, losing control of his metaphor.

"Maybe not so," said the Lady. She had nabbed Arthur's list of magical folk and spell services while he was lost in thought. "I see one name on this list you haven't crossed out. Maybe she'll help."

Arthur froze in fear. "No, anyone but her. Anyone but her!"

"Sorry, dumbo," she said, returning the list to its stuttering owner. "Looks like you're out of options." At that, the Lady of the Lake started laughing at Arthur like a soda factory worker on break.

Alas, the king's temper got the best of him and he later regretted his funny reply.

"Better out of options than out of lake!" Arthur paused, realizing his mistake. "Uh-oh."

And with that solid burn on her home life, the Lady had had quite enough of Arthur. She grabbed what was left of the lake and dealt both king and horse a good muddy splashing. Dodging the biggest lumps of goop, Arthur said his goodbyes and raced away on slippery hooves.

Chapter 6
Morgana's House

Arthur was not the kind of king to give up on a quest after the first hiccup. He was not the kind of king to give up after a hundred hiccups, a few loud coughs, and one great big sneezing fit. This described his journey quite well as it had rained often.

By now, Arthur had travelled to the opposite side of Britain. The king had gone very far north and very far from Camelot. He was so far away that his map was now nothing more than a blank beige slab covered in many question marks. The map had run out a few squares ago. The last thing it showed was a pretty picture of a giant octopus trying to drag a ship beneath the waves. Arthur had passed him days ago. So, from then on, the king had planned his route by either flipping a coin or closing his eyes and pointing. The last few miles had been guesswork at best. Still, Whiffy hadn't fallen off a cliff, which meant, in his own mind, Arthur's method was working.

But still the king would not give. After all, Sir Softpaws was his faithful friend and companion, (well, not too faithful. He liked to visit neighbouring castles and help himself to cat treats and extra strokes. But for a cat, he was loyal and true). Now, thanks to Merlin, he breathed fire and was bigger than ten horses. Only the foolish, blind, or reckless would dare to stroke him. Worrying about how his poor cat would survive in a world without strokes, Arthur galloped onwards until he reached yet another magical forest.

Unlike previous magical forests, this was not a forest where you went to get in touch with nature. Screaming trees and their black branches, and the constant bellowing of skull-shaped smoke told even stupid travellers they weren't welcome here. Woodland critters who once lived here had left for greener pastures and much less bottomless pits and giant spiders. Not even a dark lord would be seen in a place so bad. Few who entered this forest were ever seen again and it wasn't because they found a good place to build a bowling green.

There was also the issue of cluckawort.This place was

loaded with the terrible shrub. Cluckawort is a strange weed. Something in its smell drives pheasants and peasants to madness (but for some reason has no effect on pigeons or anybody who owns a holiday home). One whiff of the stuff and things become quite crazy. Whether it's using their beaks or pitchforks, the infected attack the nearest person without rhyme nor reason. It takes many days for them to calm down.

Once, there had been an outbreak in Camelot (Merlin was trying to make a cheap skin cream). Both bird and commoner rose up and rebelled against Arthur every single day. For once, the king didn't deserve it, but still they set Camelot Coffee on fire and he went without coffee for a whole month. Thankfully when the weed had been cleared up and dumped in another kingdom, life quickly returned to normal. Soon there was the usual mild grumbling and Arthur continued getting poorly laid eggs.

Arthur had only one name left on his list. It was a name he hated reading, let alone meeting the name's owner face to face and turning up on her doorstep to ask for a favour. This person was a magical genius and, if begged nicely on hands and knees, might undo some of Merlin's damage. But using her was quite risky. She was not to be trusted.

The genius may have the power to restore Sir Softpaws to his normal size but she was unpredictable. Things could go off the rails quicker than you could say 'whoops'. If she decided to cause trouble, the trouble would not be small. We would not be talking about the kind of magical mishap where all the milk in Camelot suddenly turns sour. No, Camelot would likely be invaded by a plague of mad vampire bats followed by a stormcloud raining fire that made every knight grow three extra heads. Arthur shuddered when he thought about the pain, expense and shortages of helmets. Even the name of this sorcerer was sinister: Morgana Le Fey.

Arthur thought he was getting nearer to Morgana's house when things started to get strange. The shrubs slowly changed from a pleasant patchwork of fields into hedges of doom with scary roses. The road ahead became harder. Its stones were broken and cracked. Even Whiffy the horse stumbled and lost his footing a couple of times. So the king was forced to slow his progress to a gentle trot. He chose a side path surrounded by fewer spiky hedges. Unfortunately, to his dismay, Arthur realized too late that they were choked with cluckawort.

All of a sudden, from behind the hedges, there came a crazed quacking sound. The leaves rustled and something feathery shot out and latched onto Arthur's face. It let out a wild hoot, flapped its wings backwards, and pecked him very hard on the nose.

"Argh! It's a pheasant!" yelled the king. "Help! Help! Cluckawort!"

The bird let out a strained gobbling cry to his friends. Another pheasant joined him, then a third, then twelve. Soon, Arthur and Whiffy were beset by many crazy birds.

Before the king knew it, he had been knocked off his horse to the ground with a feathery thump. Now he was wrestling with an uncountable number of mad pheasants. It was very different from when Arthur wrestled a mad peasant. That had happened last month when he pushed in line at a puppet show. This time it wasn't Arthur's fault. These loony birds had come out of nowhere and randomly started attacking him.

"What ya doing rollin' round the floor with my birds?" asked a voice who happened to be passing by. "It drives them mad, ya' know. Don't make me too happy neither." A man pushed his way through the hedges. He was tall, strong, and scratching himself with his heavy axe.

"I wasn't –" began the king as the pheasant flapped its way free from his clutches. "I mean, it's not what it looks like. They started it." He pointed at the birds who stared daggers at him. The burly man gathered every bird in one big arm and raised Arthur to his feet using the other.

"I don't sees many strangers 'round these parts. I be taking then you're lost," the man said while giving the king a good dusting down. Then he picked a loaf of bread from his bushy beard and began to feed the birds.

"Thank goodness you're here," said Arthur, thankfully. "I feared that I was going to be pecked to bits."

"Have no fear, stranger," said the bearded breaded man. "You knows what they says... a stranger be a friend you 'aven't met yet." He harshly picked at his earhole before calling out. "Pa! Ma! Cousin Humphrey! Come on out an' meet me friend, the stranger."

Three equally old, mouldy and cabbagey figures emerged

from the hedges to say 'howdy'. The king assumed they were Pa, Ma and Cousin Humphrey. After exchanging handshakes, the trio picked up the loose pheasants and returned them home. Home was a chicken coop on wheels meaning they could take the birds from place to place without much bother. Together, they were a family of travelling pheasant farming woodfolk. Meeting new people or anyone with a different nose or surname was a welcome delight.

"Why don' ya join us for a spot of tea?" suggested Ma. "I won't be taking 'no' for an answer.""

"If Ma don't make the best tea in Britain, then my name ain't Cousin Humphrey!" said Cousin Humphrey. The family shared a hearty laugh. Arthur didn't get the joke.

So they all rested. Ma brewed a pot of tea using the nearest herbs and leaves. The refreshing brew was mostly enjoyed by Whiffy the horse who finally drank his first drink in eight days. (Arthur hasn't been near water often since the Lady of the Lake incident). After they had at least three cups of tea each, Arthur felt he knew his guests well enough to ask for some information.

"I'm looking for someone who lives in these woods," said the king. "She's very special."

"Well, we're all lookin' for someone special."

Cousin Humphrey's eyes glittered with dreams of romance. "Why don't you try the disco instead?"

"I mean, she's a talented witch," snorted the king. Suddenly he didn't want to drink tea anymore.

The family talked among themselves until Pa raised a finger. "You must be meanin' that gingerbread witch. She's the only witch around these parts… I hope."

"Gingerbread witch?" coughed Arthur in disbelief. "There's no way Morgana would ever call herself The Gingerbread Witch. She's far too proud."

"Well, we calls her that Gingerbread Witch," answered Ma. "It's cause of all that gingerbread she bakes."

"Lives in a gingerbread house, she does," said the woodsman with a blocked nose.

"All's I knows is she's no friend of the pheasant!" snorted Cousin Humphrey. He picked out a plump bogey and spat it on the ground.

"If I'm being honest," chuckled Arthur, "after today,

pheasants are no longer in my good books."

The king waited for a laugh, but none came. He even gave a small chuckle to start everybody rolling but the others just sat there and scratched themselves. In their coop, the pheasants slowly started to itch and twitch once again.

"Oh they's alright when you gets to know them. I keeps them birds safe myself," said the woodsman. "Pheasants can get mighty strange around here. Of course, only if they's exposed to that cluckawort..."
He began to cough and pink blotches grew over his face.

Arthur suspected something was going very wrong before him. "Tell me…" he began. His eyes were wide in fear as he clutched at Whiffy's reigns. "Do you have a holiday home?"

"I can't say that I does, rich stranger," replied the man. His eyes were now an interesting shade of pink. Looking at the family, Arthur could now see their clothes were rags and they were covered in dirt. There was not a penny to their name.

"Sure, I'm not that well off when it comes to money," said the man. "But I's wealthy if you're talking family. There's me, me old man, old ma, and Cousin Humphrey. Ain't I right ma?" The woodsman threw his axe into a nearby tree to drive his point home.

Ma agreed and started pulling out her hair. Pa gave a hearty chortle before walking like a crab. Meanwhile, Cousin Humphrey screamed into his own shoes.

"Just gotta keep away from that blasted cluckawort," said Cousin Humphrey.

"Ma? What's in this here tea? Hurghleyburggle?"

"Oh no!" muttered Arthur. "Poisoned by peasants!!!"

"Grar groo mulch bragh!" spluttered the family, now maddened by Ma's tea – which Arthur realised must have been sweetened with a couple of spoonfuls of powered cluckawort, instead of sugar. There was a loud crash. Arthur saw that the pheasants had tipped over their coop. With the doors now open, the mad pheasants broke out of their cages and joined the peasants, saying "Cluck!" with considerable menace.

Only then did Arthur fully realize the trouble he was in. Throwing the pot of tea at them and missing by a good yard, he jumped on Whiffy and began to flee. Soon the king was in full flight once more, but this time he was trying to escape a crazy crowd of pheasants and peasants.

Chapter 7
Witches, Biscuits and Dipsticks

Arthur galloped through the fearful forest for what seemed like hours (a bird had stolen his watch earlier) until, at last, he came across the place he dreaded. Through the trees with scary faces, the king could just about see its bright orange walls and smell its calories. This was a gingerbread cottage caked in marzipan and held together with little more than fudge, caramel and the hope that it would never ever rain.

With a heavy gulp in his throat, Arthur climbed off Whiffy and approached the gingerbread cottage alone. He found the gate was locked and also made of jelly beans. It was unlikely there would be a key that wasn't jelly beans as well. Arthur groaned as he struggled to climb over the garden fence of hardened liquorice. When he finally landed on the other side, his foot got stuck in a toffee hedge, causing him to trip and land face down in a nearby pond. The pond was filled with strawberry milkshake and whipped cream lilypads.

Humbled and sticky, Arthur walked down a path pebbled with humbugs and fruit gum flowers before reaching Morgana's front door and pressing its creampuff doorbell. The king waited as he prepared himself for a difficult chat. Normally, he felt braver on a full stomach. So Arthur chomped down on a garden gnome made of honeycomb for courage. Weirdly enough, a mouthful of sweets would make chatting more difficult.

"Go away!" yelled a cracked voice through the peanut butter intercom.

"Mnworbama?" said Arthur, spitting crumbs everywhere. "Is that you?"

The sweetie-studded door swung open and out came Morgana Le Fey. The world-famous witch with a toxic talent for treachery was exactly as Arthur remembered her. She had the exact same scowl as before, the exact same temper too. Now her exact same wand pointed at his head.

"Morgana. What a pleasant surprise," stammered Arthur nervously.

"Surprise? You visited me, dumb-dumb," said Morgana. "Besides, it's 'Gingerbread Witch' these days. Better for business. What do you want, King Farter?"

Arthur cringed at his childhood nickname, but he was a king on a mission. Sweetly, he replied "Well Guinevere and I were talking and we thought who do we know who knows magic? And I said, why not..."

"Save it, iron pants!" snapped Morgana. "I heard all about your cat problems from the Lady of the Puddle. The answer's no, so don't even bother asking."

There was an awkward silence. The awkward silence continued awkwardly. At last, the awkward silence was awkwardly ended when Arthur tried again with the charm.

"I'd be happy if he was only the size of a double bed. So long as my cat can fit indoors again."

"Be off with you!" cried the witch, slamming the door so hard that an evil gummy bear fell from the roof. The enchanted sweet looked annoyed. It pointed a finger at Arthur bitterly. Then, with a grunt, he climbed up Morgana's creeping ivy (strawberry laces) back to his original position.

"Morgana, wait!" shouted Arthur. Just then, an idea popped into his head. But like most of Arthur's recent ideas, it was no help to his quest. It was just another nickname for the Lady of the Lake – 'Senorita Splash' (it seemed so obvious now).

"Well I think that went as well as planned," thought the king. He turned heel and returned to the gate where he'd tied up Whiffy, (the horse was surrounded by robbers who had meant to steal him, but had instead passed out from his smell). "Maybe if I put Sir Softpaws on a strict exercise plan, he might lose so much weight... he might lose a little height too."

Slowly but surely, Arthur realized he was no longer alone. A sudden fear took over as he heard strange noises behind him. The king turned, feeling a cold chill running down his spine. What Arthur saw robbed him of many good nights' sleep to come. It was the peasant family with Cousin Humphrey waiting for him. They were surrounded by flocks of crazed pheasants. With foam dripping from their mouths, each bird had a crazy look about it. Arthur gaped at the red rings around the pheasants' eyes. They stood and flapped and stared back at Arthur without blinking.

"Uh-oh!" said the king. He was right to say so.

Sharing a common goal, the crazy gang crept towards Arthur as their teeth chattered from the Cluckawort. Every step and stumble forward meant a step closer to his doom. Not even the protective fumes from Whiffy could stop them. Nobody was around to save him. At that, Arthur dropped to his knees and started praying to anyone listening. Thankfully, the king would live to ruin another day. A voice cried out--

"Oh no! Peasants! Stay away from my cottage." It was Morgana Le Fey, frightened homeowner.

Seeing the treasure of tasty treats available, the Cluckawort mob weighed up their options and decided to change their target. The witch's home was probably a better peck and bite than any part of Arthur. In one movement, the mob rushed Morgana's house while Arthur hid behind his stinky horse. A frenzy quickly broke out. Everybody was pecking and chewing and chomping and nipping and scratching and gorging and gobbling. Morgana was able to turn many of them into toads, but their numbers were too great (including Cousin Humphrey who ribbeted with joy at the thought of living in a pond made from milkshakes). Soon the witch owned nothing that didn't have freshly-made bite marks. With the chaos all around him, even Arthur got a little hungry and helped himself to a chocolate biscuit cornerstone. By the time he swallowed the snack, the gingerbread cottage had collapsed in a sugary landslide.

"Crumbs! I mean… oh no!" exclaimed the accident-prone king. "Back to Camelot, Whiffy, with haste. It appears my quest has met with full farty failure."

"Neigh!" agreed the smelly horse.

With no more famous or trustworthy magicians left in Britain, Arthur felt like this was a good time to return to Camelot and try something else. So they galloped away, ignoring the angry shouts coming from the pile of sticky rubble where Morgana's cottage used to be.

Chapter 8
It Gets Worse

Arthur returned to Camelot to find the drawbridge missing. No doubt, the cat was to blame. What's worse, nobody was in a hurry to let him inside. After searching for many hours to find a way back into his kingdom, the king chose to climb the outer tower and slip in through its highest window. Thankfully, while he was away, Sir Softpaws had been using the rocky pillar as a scratching post. This left a trail of craggly claw marks and deep notches in the stonework which just about gave Arthur a firm grip.

The podgy king puffed and groaned as he journeyed ever upwards. Soon he was high above people's houses and had overtaken a cloud or two. No matter how high he climbed, Arthur's little pot belly prevented him from getting a good look at the ground below and making himself dizzy. When he was finally out of puff, the king found a small nook in the wall and decided to take a short rest (only after booting out a family of crows first who didn't want to share their nest with him). There, he could see all of Camelot below.

By now, the Softpaws fandom had really gotten out of hand. Pictures of the cat covered Camelot. His moggy mug was everywhere; on banners, on signs, on statues, painted on the cobblestones, on dinner plates, on cups and mugs, on shields, on walls in crayon, even on the front of peasants' dirty tunics. People sang songs. Old women knitted his likeness on cushions. There was a cat themed sockpuppet theatre putting on shows that were well into their third week. In the town square was the real Sir Softpaws. The townspeople were feeding him a deep fried whale, which he swallowed in one satisfying mouthful. The cat received a warm applause as he burped up a whale-sized skeleton.

Arthur was jealous. He had been their ruler for many years. He still longed for a time where his subjects could be counted on to feed him large amounts of fish. He hoped they would also applaud him when his dinner was done. Sometimes, Arthur thought, life was unfair. He lacked the cat's star power and it seemed Softpaws would not be a one-hit wonder. The king humphed and started to climb once again. Nearing the end of his journey, he slipped in through a window headfirst and knocked over a table full of potions.

Here was Merlin's laboratory. This time, there was daylight. Alone and free to explore, Arthur played "royal detective" (it was great fun, but the king would never tell). He searched every corner of the wizard's lair, brushing off every shelf, reading every dusty book, poking every uncleaned cauldron, and getting into a scrape with some stubborn spiders. Somewhere among Merlin's mess there was a clue why the conjuror had turned Sir Softpaws into a lumbering giant. Any secret recipes for cat shrinking would have been perfect and would have ended the book here, but Arthur had no such luck. Instead, Arthur found nothing except hundreds of bottles of hair dye, many unfinished lunches, and an unconvincing drawing of a peacock.

Mildly miffed, the king put his feet up on Merlin's desk. Opening a drawer, he spotted a folder crammed with many crumpled papers. They all contained the shifty wizard's side projects and business pitches to rival kingdoms. Luckily, Arthur didn't understand any of their magical formulas, recipes, or Merlin's crude doodles. Other post-it parchments were more interesting. One sure-fire winner read, 'idea for King Patisserie of Cake Kingdom: "Sword in the scone."' Another one was for "Sword in the throne", a shop that sold unusually pointy furniture. On a third was scribbled "Sword on the loan? Play tennis with Lancelot this Saturday. Bring money!!!".

With the exception of a tavern where they served exotic drinking potions named "Excali-bar", most of Merlin's ideas seemed to run along the theme of swords getting stuck in something. Arthur sighed. His pet wizard had passed his peak a long time ago. Although Arthur was still cross with the dirty rotten sneak, he didn't have the heart to banish him from the kingdom. After all, no one could tell a good knock knock joke quite like old Merlin.

At that moment, a manly figure of a man sporting well-polished armour, skin softer than double cream, and an A-list haircut, burst into the room. He had an uneasy expression on his incredibly handsome face.

"There you are, your highness. Bad news, I fear. Stinking

bad awful news." It was Sir Lancelot.

"What is it now, Lancelot?" yelped the king, stashing the 'Excali-bar' blueprints down his chainmail vest. "If I hear anything more about that giant cat…"

"No, no, no, sire! It's not about the cat. It's an invasion!"

"Of cats?" Arthur thought about hiring an army of dogs and putting a ban on flea powder.

"I wish, my lord," The knight's eyes briefly twinkled. "With regret, I must inform you this is a normal invasion of humans with swords, sharp sticks and the like. Not half as cuddly."

Arthur leaned back and sulked. In Camelot it was one disaster from the next. Dealing with these problems was tiring and gave the king no time to work on his stamp collection.

"OK Lancelot, I'll bite," growled Arthur in a kingly voice. "Who dares invade my kingdom?" .

"Enemies, sire! Enemies!"

"Obviously! But who? Names, Lancelot! Names!" asked the king. A vein began to throb on his forehead like a belly dancing snake.

Lancelot looked around Merlin's filthy room to make sure nobody was listening. Nobody at all.. None of Merlin's 'listening ravens'. No eavesdropping lab rats. No frogs wearing crowns who probably worked for other kingdoms.

"My Lord," he said, followed by a long pause. "Do you remember your last birthday party?"

Arthur started blankly into space and slowly nodded. His face was white with fear. This was going to be about Captain Funnynuggets. It was always Captain Funnynuggets. All Arthur's recent woes seemed to involve him somehow.

Chapter 9
What Captain Funnynuggets Did

The last royal birthday was one to remember. Normally, a king's birthday is an opportunity to protect the kingdom. It is an easy-to-follow plan to make strong friends. There aren't many rules. There aren't many ways to muck it up. First, you invite the other kings and queens of Britain over. Then you hold a great feast in your biggest banqueting hall. You put on some jesters, gobble down a hefty meal of many courses, and send everyone home happy. If the party went off without a hitch, you were unlikely to be invaded in the future.

Things had started well enough. Just as planned, Arthur had invited everyone down to Camelot in hopes of getting on their good sides. There were jesters, fire jugglers, candyfloss, king cake, and all that sort of thing. His banquet hall was clean and shiny. Many hefty courses were gobbled down. Merlin had even prepared magical 'goody-bags' for the good kings and queens to take home (before he mysteriously disappeared, of course).

The event turned into a right royal disaster when in came Captain Funnynuggets, Britain's funniest clown. Guinevere had booked him as a surprise present for her husband and to give everyone there a good old chuckle.

Now, it is often said that 'everybody loves a clown'. But the truth is that some people really don't like them and find them kind of creepy. Arthur was one of these people. When he first set eyes on Captain Funnynuggets, the king almost jumped out his chainmail. By the time the clown had moved onto balloon animals, the king was quivering like a royal jelly.

Being such a gifted performer, Captain Funnynuggets did his best to keep the show rolling along. His audience were still laughing until their belly's ached, but the birthday boy wouldn't stop throwing things at him, shouting "Begone, evil clown!" During his juggling act, Funnynuggets had to keep many balls up in the air while avoiding the swords Arthur lobbed in his direction. Thankfully, the clown was also a skilled acrobat and dodged them with ease. He even started juggling the swords and earned a much louder applause.

But the clown was running out of material fast. Since Arthur had thrown away his dancing pigeons, Funnynuggets was forced to make up his next trick on the spot. His first thought was a risky one. The clown chose to mimic Arthur being a cowardly coward. He painted himself bright yellow, made a crown of slippers, and started dancing with a wobbling plate of strawberry jelly. While everyone else fell about laughing, this made the king explode with rage. So, half way through his birthday party, Arthur had a tantrum and cancelled the clown then and there.

While Captain Funnynuggets packed his oversized novelty bags, the other kings and queens of Britain began to grumble and complain. Guinevere had promised them a clown and that was what they expected to get. A shoving match broke out between the royal guests. Tables were knocked over. Cake was thrown. Smaller knights were robbed. Sensing a crisis, the king puffed up his chest and decided to take charge of the mess. He scurried out the hall to prepare.

Later, Arthur re-entered in a red nose and white make-up and wearing one of Merlin's 'novelty robes'. For the sake of peace and birthday fun, the king would play the clown. Arthur would entertain everyone with his best jokes. He told all the jokes he knew. How King Alfalfa had hairy shoulders. How Queen Agatha smelt like rotten peaches. How King Artery had a nose shaped like a foot. Every single joke he knew. Every single one, no matter how much they booed. He was on stage for three whole hours.

When the guests were about to riot, Guinevere signalled Merlin to put an end to Arthur's disaster. The wizard magicked up some theatre curtains and instantly closed them, showing to all that the show had finished. On each curtain read 'No Refunds'. Seeing nobody but him had a sense of humour, an angry Arthur banished everyone from the party. He also denied them 'goody bags'.

The other kings of Britain had all sworn their revenge that day, but Arthur never thought they'd actually go through with it. He would later write down the incident in his diary of royal mistakes. This was now well into its twelfth volume.

Chapter 10
It Gets Worse, Much Worse

Back in Merlin's laboratory, Arthur gulped as he recalled that most horrible of birthdays. It was even worse than the party before, where he introduced his new game 'pin the tail on the wolf' and briefly lost control of Camelot to some sore, furry moon-howlers. For now, all the king could do was whimper, "Oh no!"

"Oh yes," replied Lancelot. "It's them, my lord. And there's a lot of them!" To prove his point, he slammed a stack of opened letters on Merlin's desk. Each one had menacing handwriting and went into great detail what each writer wished to do to King Arthur.

Arthur sat and weighed up outcomes in his mind. There was a small chance that everyone would forget where Camelot was and attack another kingdom. Maybe their generals would march the soldiers into a river full of hungry crocodiles. It wasn't completely stupid for the enemy army to simply change their minds and realize Arthur wasn't such a bad guy after all. The king crossed his fingers for any of these miracles (just in case).

But then the king felt a numbing tingle across his feet. He peered down to see a queue of Merlin's laboratory spiders. Their bags were packed and they were slowly exiting the room through a crack in the wall. It looked like they were ready to leave the kingdom forever. This was clearly a bad omen.

Arthur turned to his star knight. When things were hairy, Lancelot was your man. He had a winning streak longer than Merlin's criminal record. "Lancelot, can't you… you know… just… be a pal and deal with it?" the king pleaded. "Five minutes of sword slapping with you and the problem will be history."

Lancelot sighed as he put a book about 'inner peace' back on the shelf. "Would that I could, sire. It's true, most true, my knightly deeds are known throughout the land and my handsome face has 'hero' written all over it. But alas, not even I could overcome enemies with so great a number."

"A great number of enemies, you say?" asked Arthur in a

rather worried tone.

"I'm afraid so, sire. There's an oath going around. Many kings have signed it. Something about getting revenge, storming the castle, eating your private sweet collection, yada yada yada. I couldn't read any further..."

"Why not?" gulped the king. "Was it too terrifying?"

"Not for me," said Lancelot. "I was running late for an appointment with my hairdresser." He flashed a streak of neatly trimmed blonde hair. "But I gathered it was a long oath. In short, they are about as mad as a flock of mad pheasants on a lake of cluckawort."

Arthur thought for a second. Maybe he could treat himself to a second birthday and make good. He still had most of the cake leftover and many of the jugglers were still chained up in his dungeon. With a thorough cleaning, the banquet hall would be ready in no time.

"Um, about Captain Funnynuggets," began the King, his voice wobbling. "Is it too late too..."

"Yes, your highness," said Lancelot "I'm sorry to say the clown is booked up for the next three years. After all, he is the best birthday clown in the land."

Now, Arthur was out of ideas. "I see," he said. "So war it is, then?"

"It would seem so, sire," replied the knight. "Shall I prepare your escape chariot?"

"No good! Sir Softpaws took a nap in the front seat and now the thing has been crushed to matchsticks." Arthur sighed as he remembered the places his dear little kitten used to sleep. He sighed louder as he remembered the safe places his escape chariot used to take him.

Without a fast vehicle to flee danger, Arthur was forced to rise to the occasion. He stood to his feet and issued his orders. "Time to assemble the knights," he declared.

"Of the roundtable?" added Lancelot, looking hopeful.

"Sure, them. Anyone. No time to be picky, Lancelot. Bring everyone you can find!" said Arthur. "The school of learner knights. The squad of half-trained squires. The archery refresher class. Knights of the Side Table. The league of junior basket weavers. Anyone who can bring their own pole axe. And find out why the boy scouts won't return my letters!"

Lancelot nodded, turned in a smooth motion, and cantered

out the room on his mission. His blonde hair was flowing in the wind like the world's finest creamed corn.

Moments later, in marched Sir Gawain (whose hair was average at best). In a state of shock, he rushed towards the king, tripped over a stool and landed with a painful bump on both knees. "Sire, terrible news! Terrible, terrible news!" He declared, rubbing his ouching legs.

"Don't tell me, Gawain, I already know," said Arthur calmly raising a hand, "Many armies approach. Badly outnumbered. No hope of victory. Just another Wednesday in Camelot."

"Sire?" Gawain looked confused as he slowly climbed to his feet and nursed his boo boos.

"No need to panic, my clumsy knight. Lancelot told me everything," continued the king. "He's gathering every hero, warrior, ruffian, and anyone with access to a big club or what have you. All is well… I hope."

"No Sire, that's not–" But Gawain was interrupted by yet more royal rambling.

"In a few days' time, we'll send that nasty army packing with their tails between their legs. And the battle shall be called 'The Mighty Booting of the Butt starring King Arthur the Great." Arthur sighed and imagined himself in a very big history book with pictures.

"It's not that," said Gawain. "Not that at all." The knight came closer to the king and kept his voice low. "It's about the royal cat…"

"What now?" moaned Arthur.

"Well, your highness," began Gawain. "It seems Sir Softpaws is… well he's... he's… he's..."

"He's what?" Arthur exclaimed. "He's got a cute button nose? Coughed up a hairball? Destroyed my private garden? Forgotten he's house-trained? What is it?" Arthur braced himself for the worst, which was becoming a frequent guest in these parts.

"Sire... he's magic." At that, there was a crash of lightning. Merlin's magical jacuzzi was playing up again. The room then began to smell of lemons. It wasn't all bad news.

The king rolled his eyes. "I know he's magic," Arthur snapped. "Sure, breathing fire is impressive for a cat, but let's not go overboard. There's no more magic in him than a fluffy, milk-drinking dragon."

"That's where you're wrong, sire. While you've been away, his magical powers have been growing and growing! Now, he's two card tricks and a top hat short of going on tour and entertaining every child in Britain!"

"Rats!" said Athur, not sure how to take this news. "How magical is Sir Softpaws now, exactly?"

"Very magical, sire. Very very magical," said Gawain. "I've been following him all day. At breakfast, one nod of his head and the town's sausages came alive and started to dance. Following that, he took a trip to the park and with a wave of his paw turned the duck pond into a volcano. Now half of camelot smells like roasted duck. I've seen him breathe ice with his fishy cat breath, make himself invisible and just now, he sneezed and it started snowing. I tell you, that is one magical cat."

Wrapping up his story, Gawain coughed up a fur ball. It changed into a butterfly and flew away. "See? That's never happened before."

"I see." Arthur saw.

"And it's only getting worse. I think his litter tray has become an enchanted portal. We've been getting letters of complaint. At least we think they are. Nobody understands their language."

Arthur smiled. In his head, he added up all the money he would save on kitty litter.

"Good!" said the king. "Tell the Knights of the Rectangular Tray to return his litter tray sand back to Camelot's beaches."

"Very good, my lord. But I must add, we're going bankrupt trying to feed him," said Gawain.

"Double rats! Spoke too soon," muttered Arthur. "That'll teach me to think positive!"

Gawain looked around the room with menace on his mind. He leaned in close, careful to whisper his idea secretly, but he only really succeeded in making the king's ear wet.

"If you want, sire... when nobody's looking... I can slay him. I have a pretty strong track record when it comes to slaying," said Sir Gawain. He winked. "Remember?"

"Don't we all know it?" replied Arthur. His mind raced back to when the Camelot zoo had been filled with wildlife.

"Gawain, do not slay my cat and that's an order. If you want to keep your head on your shoulders."

Gawain rubbed his neck for good measure and his plans to help the 'kitty-cat crisis' ended as quickly as they had begun.

"Right-ho," chuckled the knight. He whistled and skipped as he left the room, before running down the corridor to safety.

But then, when Arthur thought his troubles were over, in came Sir Bors. He charged into the room like a wild boar who'd just found the gift shop in Piggy Hogland. Like all the knights today, he was very worried.

"Sire, terrible news!" he yelled in a panic. "It's the worst news I've ever heard!"

"Can it wait?" sighed Arthur, who was done with today.

"No, sire, it cannot wait," insisted the flustered knight! "I ran here as fast as my feet could carry me."

Arthur had clearly hurt his feelings.

"No, Bors. No more. That's enough bad news for today. Even kings deserve a rest now and then."

At that, Arthur opened the secret fridge Merlin kept under his desk and helped himself to the wizard's stash of magical sodas. In one gulp, he downed the fizzy liquid inside and suddenly sprouted rabbit ears.

"Everything's under control," said Arthur, scratching his bunny tail. "And while you're at it – get me a carrot!" Saying these words, he hopped away and was chased around the castle by a pack of local dogs.

Chapter II
A Long Boring Chapter About Planning

Finding himself changed into a rabbit was a hassle. The life of a bunny certainly had its problems. For one, Arthur couldn't curse and complain about Merlin, no matter how hard he tried. All the king could do was helplessly twitch his cute little button nose in anger. But once he got over the shock of suddenly enjoying lettuce, Arthur's last few hours as a rabbit had been the best of his life. He went on many adventures around Camelot's vegetable patches. But they were too amazing to be written down in one simple children's book. Sadly but slowly Merlin's potion wore off and Arthur returned to human form once more, but the king would forever keep an allotment in the castle's back garden. Missing his fluffy tail, big ears, and new found love of hopping, Arthur was back to normal (or at least as 'normal' as Arthur was).

Now he was a king on a mission. Arthur marched toward a very special room near the back of Camelot castle. This was where the world-famous Round Table was kept. He had ordered the oddly-shaped table from a Swedish furniture maker. The king was fed up with his knights and their bickering. They were constantly boasting over who could lift the heaviest weights, or who could fight the most bears, or rescue the most princesses from the tallest towers. But what they argued about most of all was who should sit closest to the king at the important end of the table.

So the Round Table was built round to put a stop to all this squabbling – that way everyone sat in equally important places (plus Arthur kept hurting himself on sharp table corners). 'That's Swedish design genius for you,' Arthur thought. His chair was bigger than everyone else's and it was also studded with jewels.

As Arthur entered the keep and made his way towards the room, Old Bede, the gatekeeper, greeted him in the usual manner. He pulled out his sword and stopped the king in his tracks. "Stop in the name of the King!" he ordered, waving his sword near Arthur's face.

"It's me, you twit!" said Arthur. "Can we skip the security questions today? I'm in a hurry."

The gatekeeper shook his head. "State your name and business!"

"Arthur Pendragon, King of Camelot," muttered Arthur. He knew that there was no point in fighting the system. "My business is not to make my day worse."

"Very good, Martha," replied the gatekeeper. He wrote "Martha" on a brightly coloured name badge and slapped it onto the king's breastplate with a merry chuckle. "Just doing my job. Hope you understand. There's a lot of strange folk going around these parts, causing all sorts of trouble, they are."

"Yes, yes," replied the king, preparing to be sarcastic. "You've got to be extra careful when there's strange folk about. No need to worry about the large magical cat destroying Camelot." He pointed to a wall that had been knocked over earlier.

"Sir Softpaws? Oh, there's a cat after my own heart. Can you believe he took a nap in my garden? My garden! Ate the fishpond bare. I tell you it's not every day you meet a celebrity."

"Not even the king?"

"Meh, I see enough of his ugly mug on the money."

"Just let me pass… please," Arthur huffed as he barged through the door.

Arthur's heart was heavy as he entered the Round Table Room. So few knights had assembled that Percival and Galahad had to remove the table's middle section. In the middle of the oval table was a large pile of scrolls. They contained apologies from the knights who weren't there. The king opened the scrolls and read each one in turn. The excuses ranged from 'Sorry I'm out on a quest' to 'My hamster must be woken with true love's kiss' and 'I'm following my dream to be a court jester.' Sadly, these were Arthur's more sensible knights who had clearly gotten wind of the huge unbeatable army. The warriors gathered here were nothing more than "glory-hunting idiots", or as they were now known 'the Knights of the Oval Table.' The bickering had started once again.

"Is this everyone?" sighed the king as he climbed onto his big chair. Its gold shined and jewels sparkled. The knights sat at their usual stools and continued to quietly argue.

"Knights of the Round Table," Arthur began. "You are gathered here today to answer a most grave and serious threat to Camelot."

"Grave and serious? That's not good," muttered the knights to one another.

"It is super serious," said Arthur. "Tell them Lancelot!"

Lancelot sprang to his feet in glee. "Thank you sire, it would be my honour." The wonder knight leapt onto the table, crashing his steel boots down on its polished planks. Watched by all gathered, he began his epic speech.

"My fellow knights," he said. "There is an army approaching the kingdom from far and wide and bigger than any I have seen. I have received word they are led by four kings, all mighty warriors. There is King Arteur from the French kingdom of Camembert. King Oither from the Lake District's Ca'elot kingdom. King Halfer from the dwarf kingdom probably near some mountains. And let us not forget King Arty Whatsisname from somewhere or other. Even though they come from every piece of the map, they share one goal in common: to get revenge on our king for being an ungrateful meanie on his last birthday."

"Hey!" objected Arthur. "We don't know that for sure." But the knights simply turned to one another and nodded. They loved Captain Funnynuggets.

Lancelot continued. "These fearsome kings lead an army in the millions of millions. This army is so large and heavy that the British isles are now on a slight slant. Every field they march through becomes squelchy mud. Every vegetable patch is turned into a floor salad. Among their ranks are many fierce and dangerous creatures. Trolls. Dragons. Skeletons. Dark knights. Goblins. Lawyers. Ghosts. War Hamsters. Demons. Chickens of Doom. Griffins. Things with lots of teeth and some monsters so terrifying that our scientists have been too frightened to name them."

"Thank you, Lancelot. I think they get the idea," growled Arthur. He guessed correctly that Lancelot's speech had put the other knights a little on edge. Sure enough, every face was pickle green.

The king rose to speak. "Knights of the Round Table, let me be blunt. Our wickets are sticky. Canoes are without paddles. Ducks are no longer in a row. Every egg can't find its basket. Local dogs are tap-dancing and playing the clarinet. In short, we're in big trouble. Any questions?"

Sir Bedivere raised his hand. "Our enemies. Are they hiring?" he asked.

"That's the kind of talk we're trying to discourage here, Bedivere," replied Arthur.

Bedivere was disappointed. He had helped a lot with Merlin's business idea ('Sword on the Loan') and been rented out to twenty eight kingdoms so far. There was good money to be made as a knight for hire (so long as you never wore the same armour twice).

"What we need," continued Arthur, "is a plan for complete and total victory! Your best ideas, please." Arthur regretted these words instantly.

"I have an idea, my liege," said Bors, raising his iron-clad hand.

"Ah, Sir Bors," called Arthur. "A sensible idea from a sensible knight!"

"Hear me, my king," began Bors in a drawling voice. "We have Sir Softpaws. Why don't we use our monster cat to frighten away the enemy? One look at him, they'll be running for the hills."

Arthur thought for a moment, then gave a grumpy frown for the ages.

"I said best ideas, Bors, not bad ideas!" he roared. "Sir Softpaws is far too sweet to be a battle cat anyway. He wouldn't harm a fly… deliberately. Besides, a great big kitten on the battlefield would be an easy target for every enemy archer."

The knights let out a disappointed grumble. Any knight will tell you that any giant creature is a useful friend on the battlefield, be it fluffy or not.

Sir Lid-shut was next to offer his thoughts. The trouble with him was that ever since Merlin had put a curse on his helmet, it had been impossible to remove. Nobody understood a word he said. Neither did anyone remember why Merlin cast such a cruel spell on Sir Lid-shut, but knowing him, it was probably revenge or a dare. The wizard was very petty.

"Puh-shh-me-lug," began Sir Lid-shut. "Vuh bem le ooo bax ridnein with monkeys."

"Very good, Sir Lid-shut, but where are we possibly going to get that many chilli peppers?"

The other knights nodded politely – but no one had the faintest idea what he was talking about.

"Mh, pie-bo!" he continued with passion. "Meste klek nip nip noop booley booley mezen dor?"

"I'm sorry, Sir Lid-shut" said Arthur with a sad face "Such a plan would have been perfect, if only we wore matching parachutes."

There were yet more plans and schemes but none worth going into detail here. Sir Gawain thought it was a bright idea to tie balloons to Camelot so they would float away to safety. Sir Percival preferred knocking down the kingdom brick by brick and rebuilding it from memory somewhere else. Sir Headstrong suggested an element of surprise by attacking everyone else's kingdom while they were out. Sir Tristan imagined they could all move to different castles and make a fresh start under fake names.

But nobody came up with a perfect plan to save Arthur's hide. A few hours later, the Knights of the Round Table felt a little gloomy and had given up pitching ideas. Without hope or escape plans, Arthur decided that it was up to him to inspire his troops.

"Knights of the Round Table! Who are we kidding?" began the king. "We are men of action, not men of planning and such. Our home is the battlefield."

The knights slowly lifted from their gloom.

"Do you fear such a large enemy? Do overwhelming odds make you quiver in your armour? Do the knights of Camelot run from danger?"

"No, but the king usually skips from it." Sir Percival was yet to be convinced.

"Not this time," returned Arthur in a heroic voice. "With our chips thoroughly cashed, with our geese thoroughly cooked, I will stand with you. For glory, my knights. For glory!"

Every eye was on the king. A new faith in them began to bloom.

"What you need is a strong leader. A leader who thinks we should defend Camelot from behind the walls so we don't all get turned to chopped chicken liver."

"Hooray!" bellowed the knights.

"A leader who doesn't need magical cats to fight his battles for him."

"Hooray!" they bellowed again.

"A king who is the king of Camelot."

"Hooray!" came another bellow.

"A king who says no more excuses!"

"Hooray!"

"Now is the time for action!"

"Hooray!"

"The thrill of glory!"

"Hooray!"

"No more time for second guesses!"

"Hooray!"

"I'm going on holiday. See you next year."

"Hoo- whuh?"

The knights were caught out by their king's cowardly change of heart. But before Arthur could make a speedy exit through the door, three of his burliest knights had blocked the way. "Drat," thought the king. "Almost got away."

He was more surprised when these knights lifted him on their shoulders and began carrying him around the room. Every man there was cheering.

Unfortunately for Arthur, his hero speech was too good. The words lit a fire in the hearts of his fighting men. They were flipped on their heads. They beat their chests. They whooped. They strutted. They butted heads. They shouted in loud shouty voices. There was no stopping them now. A fresh roar of approval echoed around the table. There was also some background roaring from latecomers.

"Our king has shown us the way," began Lancelot (he had been standing on the table the entire time). "When the enemy arrives, we shall face him in the field of battle and box his ears to kingdom come."

Sir Pokesalot joined in with his brother. "We shall gift him a few swift kicks to the behind and send him packing with our boot prints on his breeches."

"And then help ourselves to any gold he leaves behind."

Sir Cheataslot knew the game well.

"And I shall enjoy my first ever victory as a Knight of the Round Table." Sir Losealot's face glimmered with hope, until Pokesalot put an understanding hand on his brother's shoulder (of the famous "Alot" brothers, he was the weakest. His losing streak wouldn't be broken so easily.)

"Sounds wonderful. See you later." Arthur reached one more time for the doorknob, but was held back. "Rats."

"But Sire, you have the most important job of all." said Sir Gawain.

"Do I?" asked Arthur wishing for a closer knob.

"Yes, your highness," said Sir Bedivere. "It is you who must choose the leader of our charge."

"Only our king may pick his star knight to be first into battle," said Sir Tristan.

"I-shh-has-a-slug," said Sir Lid-Shut.

"That's right," said Sir Headstrong. "And the first man to charge the enemy earns the most glory."

The knights nodded in agreement. Only now did they actually agree on something.

"Do I have to?" said Arthur with a groan. "Can't you all just risk your lives at the same time."

"Sire, we are serious," said Lancelot. "I mean. I can't see the point of risking my handsome face unless there's much personal glory at the end of it."

Arthur groaned. "What do you want me to do?"

The knights fell silent and had a little think.

"Why don't we have a jousting tournament?" said Sir Galahad. "Winner gets to lead the defence of Camelot."

They all cheered while Arthur pinched his nose in frustration.

"But Lancelot is going to win anyway. He's the best knight in the land."

The knights fell silent again until one had the courage to step forward.

"This time we're feeling lucky!"

An incredibly loud 'hooray' rang throughout the castle.

Chapter 12

A Pointless Tournament Where Everyone Gets Hurt

"So, tell me one last time, why are we putting on a jousting tournament?" asked Guinevere. She shook her head quizzically as she read the programme. "Won't a lot of our knights get injured?

"Probably," cringed Arthur. He grabbed a handful of popcorn and shoved it down his angry throat.

"Now, I'm no military genius…" began the queen, "but when Camelot's about to be invaded, don't you want as many fit and healthy knights as you can get?"

"I know!" growled Arthur. He knew. "But they won't take 'no' for an answer, so we may as well grin and bear it." He wasn't grinning.

"Fair enough dear, you know best," said Guinevere, looking back at her programme. "Ooo, I can't wait for the jugglers at half time."

But Arthur had stopped listening. At that moment, he was searching the crowd for a roasted peanut seller. Fear and disappointment had made him peckish. An entire stadium had been built overnight and there was shaky woodwork wherever you looked. Terry Cotter's carpentry business (which he had on the side) had built the stadium, making the richest man in Camelot even richer (again). He had cut corners everywhere. To Arthur's annoyance, the entire joust was short on both corners and peanut sellers.

The crowd was somewhat smaller than previous tournaments. A few benches were completely empty. No more than a couple of people stood in the standing room. Perhaps Lancelot's almost-certain victory was the reason. Arthur blamed it on the newest hot ticket in town: a giant magical cat who burps rainbows.

"Oh well, at least there's always the jugglers," said Arthur. "That's something the whole family can enjoy. Isn't that right, Guinevere?... Guinevere?" But Guinevere was gone. One of her ladies-in-waiting had slipped her a message about the magical rainbow cat – who was obviously Sir Softpaws. His show started in five minutes.

Just then, a horn blew out around the arena. On a small platform, a messenger stepped forward unrolling a scroll and prepared to make a speech.

"Hear ye, hear ye, are ye ready jousting fans? The knights of Camelot will now engage in violent combat to decide who is the best – even though we all know that Lancelot is the best, eh folks?"

There was a polite ripple of clapping.

"His kingly highness, King Arthur, will now declare the games open."

"Get on with it!" yelled Arthur from the royal box. He almost choked on a peanut with rage.

"Very well. The games are… open?" The horn blew again and so the jousting began.

The first match up saw Sir Percival pitted against Sir Bors. This would not be a fair contest, not even close. Sir Bors was an excellent jouster on the back of a bad-tempered horse. Sir Percival was known to get seasick indoors.

The two knights glared at each other from opposite ends of the field and readied their weapons.

"Yaa!" roared Sir Bors aiming his long lance like a true professional.

"Neigh!" agreed Sir Bors's horse (try saying that to yourself a few times).

Arthur dropped the royal handkerchief and the match began.

"Oh no, not again," thought Sir Percival. "Why must I always--" But he didn't have time to finish his thoughts. The next thing he knew, Bors's lance had whacked him harder than a frozen chicken leg and sent him flying from his saddle. Percival sailed a good fifteen metres into the air and landed face-first in a trough of water.

"Blub!" sputtered Sir Percival.

"Splash!" added the trough.

"Winner of the first match," said the messenger pointing at Sir Bors, "Sir Bors!"

"I'm the winner!" called Sir Bors, stating the obvious. Meanwhile, two squires helped Sir Percival out of the water. His armour was already rusted. They would be using the big tin opener tonight.

The crowd cheered while Sir Bors celebrated. But then, the winning knight started showboating (he had always been a little bit of a show off). Waving at the crowd, Bors made his horse do tricks – star jumps, backflips, somersaults (guaranteed crowd pleasers). The pleased crowd cheered until Sir Bors was on his second victory lap. At this point, his horse had gotten utterly fed up and so he bolted. Soon, he was dragging the bragging knight feet first through a nasty stinging nettle patch and off into a nearby forest. The crowd cheered even louder.

"Next!" Arthur yelled. "We haven't got all day." Arthur didn't know it yet, but his peasants did have all day. Sensing the king's mind was elsewhere, nobody had planted a turnip or mowed a field for weeks. If they all agreed to keep quiet and not make a fuss, they wouldn't have to do a single day's work this side of Christmas.

"I'm bored! Where's Sir Softpaws?" yelled someone in the crowd.

"Bring out the magic cat!" wailed a family of peasants on the front row.

"It's just big men charging at each other with sticks. What's the point of that?" This one came from the referee who hadn't been paid today. Soon, chanting broke out from the yawning masses.

"I command you all to shush!" commanded Arthur. "Next round."

The messenger unrolled another scroll. "Next matchup: Sir Cheatsalot vs Sir Gawain."

"Sir Cheatsalot?" thought Arthur. "This ought to be good. I hope he plays by the rules."

Sir Cheatsalot was one of Lancelot's many brothers. The 'Alot' family, as everyone called them, were a family of famous knights (last chapter we met Sir Losealot who lost his joust later that day to a bag of weasels). But Sir Cheatsalot was the naughtiest 'Alot' of them all. Only last summer he'd tricked the king out of three bags of gold by selling him a moat mower. This summer it was snow insurance.

The horn sounded and the next two knights galloped towards each other on lightning hooves. The match was going to be epic! Neither knight gave half a mind to danger. The crowd were on the edge of their seats waiting for the clash of lance on shield, or even better the clash of lance on helmet, or even better better, the clash of helmet in pile of horse droppings.

But before the knights clashed, Sir Cheatsalot suddenly fell off his horse. He rolled along the ground and flopped like a tuna having a tantrum. The crowd gasped at the display, wondering what was going on. There was a hush before they all heard a cry of pain.

"Ow, ow, ow, ow, ow. My knee!" screamed Sir Cheatsalot holding the knee in both hands. He rolled around drawing attention to himself. "Oooo! Ow! Oh, I think it's broken, Gawain wins."

"But he never touched you!" cried Arthur.

"Oh, yes he did! It was an invisible strike. Very sneaky," protested the cheating knight.

"Sir Cheataslot, that's a bare faced lie!" fumed the king. The crowd began to grumble.

"Maybe it is, maybe it isn't. You can't prove it. Anyway, Ow my knee!" yelled Sir Cheatsalot.

Guards ran into the arena carrying a stretcher. When they reached Sir Cheatsalot, he hopped onto the stretcher with no problem. Quickly realizing his mistake, the 'fallen' knight fell off and rolled around again screaming at a hard to ignore volume. His acting was tremendous.

"Stop faking!" called a sharp eyed lady in the front row. "Get up and fight!"

"I'm not faking," replied Sir Cheatsalot. "I got better for a bit and then I got worse again. That's how you know my injuries are super-duper serious." He daintily got back onto the stretcher and signalled the guards to leave.

By now, everybody had figured out Cheatsalot's game and booed even louder. As Sir Cheatsalot left the field, Sir Gawain slipped him a small leather bag. The contents of the bag made a satisfying clinking sound.

"What did you just give him?" called the sharp eyed lady who was pleased to have a second line in this story. "Is that some sort of bribe?"

"Um, healing herbs," said Gawain. "A sign of good sportsmanship and no mistake!"

"Hear, hear!" bragged Cheatsalot. "I mean, ooo! Ouch!

Ouch! My poor knee!"

"Fine! Fine! Fine! I don't care anymore," yelled king Arthur "Get on with the jousting!"

And so they got on with the jousting. For hours the knights fought and fought. Many helmets got dented. Many lances got bented. Even more horses got angry and attacked their riders. To save time and printing paper, here's a short list of who beat up who:

Sir Geraint vs Sir Lancelot
Sir Gawain vs Sir Lancelot
Sir Cador vs Sir Lancelot
Sir Headstrong vs Sir Lancelot
Sirs Dagonet, Hector & Lionel vs Sir Lancelot (Lancelot was blindfolded)
Sir Beefy and Sir Bevidere vs Sir Lancelot (with an arm and a leg tied behind his back)
And finally, Everyone vs Sir Lancelot (followed by the Lancelot victory parade)

The unforgettable match of Everyone vs Sir Lancelot was also won by Lancelot, but at least everyone came a little closer than they had in previous matchups. Despite being utterly vanquished (which is a knight word meaning "stomped into dust"), the other knights felt good on the inside because their fighting skills were improving. Unfortunately, their outsides felt much, much worse as Lancelot had beaten them all to a pulp and 'shown them no quarter' (which is another knight word meaning 'gave a good thumping').

By the end of the day, no knight was in fighting shape except the winner. Everyone who won 'second place' would spend the next few weeks in hospital slowly getting their limbs unmangled. For now, they were no use to the king who had decided the best way to take the news was to stick his head between his knees and breathe heavily into a paper bag.

"I knew Sir Lancelot would win!" declared Guinevere, sitting in her chair once more. She was wearing a t-shirt that read: "I went to Camelot to see the amazing magical cat and all I got was this lousy t-shirt." On the shirt was a nice picture of Sir Softpaws shooting lasers from his eyes.

"Lancelot always wins, doesn't he?!" Arthur replied as the

paper bag exploded. "If only they listened to their king, maybe my knights might have avoided their painful fates. Why couldn't they just take a nap and sleep for most of the day like my cat?"

"Good point," said Guinevere, turning to her ladies in waiting. "Hurry girls, if we don't get across town, we'll miss Sir Softpaws's next show."

"I thought he'd finished for the day?" said the king. He pointed at Guinevere's t-shirt.

"He does three shows a day," she explained. "They keep selling out."

But seeing his queen already dash away as fast as her gown allowed, Arthur shrugged and got back to his royal duties.

"Let's get this over with," he announced and gave a signal to bring out the trophies.

A small stage was built in the middle of the arena and decorated with cheap plants (the Cotter group again). At the prize-giving ceremony, Lancelot knelt before Arthur. As was tradition, the king granted his champion with many lavish prizes worthy of the knight's glory and honour. Besides the trophies, these also included a miniature shield with the Camelot logo on it and a loyalty card for Camelot Coffee, where Lancelot's tenth cup would be free. A hush crept over the crowd as Arthur began his speech through gritted teeth.

"Sir Lancelot, as if nobody could have guessed it, you have shown yourself as the greatest of my knights in an utterly pointless tournament. Truly, you are a hero without equal which is really depressing because I could always use better heroes. In fact, your raw battle prowess is so great that the rest of my knights are drinking runny porridge through a straw. Well done, the honour of defending Camelot is yours alone while the kingdom faces certain doom. Why? Why? Why do I have to do this?" He trailed off into repeating the word 'Why?'

The crowd roared with applause ignoring their king's icy glare as he handed the big trophy to Lancelot. Arthur also gave Lancelot a sly kick to the kneecap when he thought nobody was looking. Most people watching assumed that this was part of the ceremony.

Triumphant, Lancelot turned his shiny smiling teeth to the cheering masses.

"People of Camelot," he said, annoyingly perfect. "As the finest knight in the land, your protection has fallen to me. I cannot lie, the road ahead will be long and unforgiving. But have no fear, because, with my mighty sword and glowing armour, I'll club our enemy to pudding—"

But Lancelot was suddenly cut short. Something gigantic that fell from the sky and landed with a terrible crump, whipping up a cloud of dust that covered the whole stadium.

By the time the sandy mist had died down, everyone realized their intruder was none other than Sir Softpaws. It seemed he had figured out how to teleport. Hearing the sound of cheering, he'd zipped over to see what the fuss was all about. Alas, his monstrous paw had accidentally squished Arthur's star knight and Lancelot's legs stuck out beneath his toes. Arthur gave a scream, but no sound came out.

"Get him off, get him off!" cried Sir Lancelot.

"S-s-someone bring a barrel of favourite creams!" ordered the King.

"Miaowww?" boomed the kitten, in a voice like a cannon. Luckily for everyone, cream is delicious. There was an almighty crash as Softpaws ran straight through a stadium stand and scampered after the dairy treat. Many more were crushed.

When the cat had gone, all eyes turned back to Sir Lancelot. The knight was as flat as a steel pancake and almost as round.

"Lancelot, are you alright?" asked the king, fingers crossed. He hoped Lancelot was alright.

Lancelot slowly opened his mouth to speak. "UUUUURRRRRRRR Puh Puh Puh Puh!" he groaned, spitting out large chunks of cat fur.

"Oh no! Oh no! Oh no!" cried the king. "My finest knight is injured on the eve of battle. What am I going to do now?" At worse, the 'pancaked' Lancelot could still double as a big shiny shield if tied to the castle walls. Arthur thought that could be Plan B.

Chapter 13
A Quick Reminder To Be Very Afraid

With every knight in Camelot injured and beyond repair, and Lancelot having been flattened by a flying kitten, Arthur was left alone to organise the defences of Camelot. He chose his own defences first. So the king hid in a cupboard with his hands over his eyes, pretending nobody would ever find him.

Arthur had been hiding all morning, eating a small breakfast of crusty bread and cold rainwater. Sir Softpaws had gotten wind of the secret food delivery the king had arranged and helped himself to an unexpected treat. In one well-planned night raid on the caravan, the clever cat had gobbled up an entire year's food supply. Kippers, salmon, trout, bacon and sausages all went missing in a moment. Not a single drop of milk remained anywhere in the castle, even though Arthur had read somewhere that milk from cows was actually supposed to be bad for cats. Sir Softpaws was keeping a balanced diet and a very healthy appetite. Arthur was kind of starting to go off him.

"Arthur? What are you doing in there?"

It was Guinevere. She knocked on the wooden door softly, careful not to wreck her poor husband's nerves.

"Eeeek! How did you find me?" came a muffled reply from the bedroom cupboard.

"I can hear your chainmail shaking." The queen was right. It sounded like a rattlesnake learning to play a steel drum.

"Leave me alone. I'm a very very sad king!" called the king.

"Come on Arthur, things aren't so bad," offered Guinevere.

"Yes, they are," he stopped. "It doesn't get any worse than this."

With a high pitched creak, the cupboard opened slightly and a trembling hand emerged holding a note. Guinevere snatched it from Arthur and began to read.

Dear So-called King Arthur,

Rotten luck about your soldiers! Sounds like a very full hospital. Still, knights will be knights, eh? Tut-tut, there I go again, rambling like always. Honestly, with the price of ink these days, I'm a stinker. Anyhoo, just a friendly note to say our army is only a couple of days' march away (as the crow flies). When we reach Camelot, no mercy, give up all hope, yada yada yada etc. And hey! The crows will probably be too FAT to fly after the terrible deeds we have planned for YOU! (See drawings below)

Yours with a soon-to-be-mashing

All your enemies (est. 27,946,255 and counting. New friends every day.)

P.S. We've sent our interior designer (Clive) to come and give the castle a makeover. The first thing we'll do is chuck out that ridiculous circle table of yours.

"Looks like they're deadly serious," moaned the queen. She nibbled her fingernails.

A knocking pair of knees could be heard from the kingly cupboard.

"Looks like I was wrong," moaned the queen again. She nibbled at her knuckles.

The knocking knees grew louder and the kingly cupboard began to wobble.

"Looks like... Budge up Arthur! Queens need hiding places too."

"No way. This cupboard is for kings only!" grumbled Arthur, flicking a boot and slamming the door shut with a royal raspberry. He spent the rest of the day in hiding.

Chapter 14
Along Came Greeny

The next day Camelot received a strange visitor who liked laughing his head off.

"Ha, ha, ha ha!" it boomed. "Ha, ha, ha, ha!"

The visitor and his horse jumped over the castle walls in a single leap and raced around the kingdom. Everywhere he went, people could hear his manic laughter. He went to the public park and hugged every tree. Then he visited the market and attacked every vegetable seller. Nobody had ever seen or heard anything like him.

But the visitor wasn't through making a scene. He single handedly invaded Camelot's keep and galloped around the halls (making a mess of the carpet). After climbing many stairs on tip-toeing hooves, his horse hoofed down the door to Arthur's bedroom. Enjoying the alarm he caused, the visitor dismounted, waving his giant axe and letting his horse bounce on Arthur's bed for fun.

With one emerald whoosh, Arthur's hiding place was destroyed. The blinding light broke apart his cupboard in a single blow, leaving the thing in sawdust and splinters. When the dust cloud had settled, there stood Guinevere, with a smile on her face, coughing loudly.

"Arthur (cough), just when you were about to give up I (cough) browsed the newspaper for warriors for hire (cough). He was the best I found (cough)."

Behind her, stood a mighty hero over ten feet tall. His hair was jade. His beard was lime. His armour was mint. His socks were the finest broccoli. Every piece of clothing he wore was greener than the last, give or take. As a bonus, his head was shaped like a swollen avocado.

"It is I, the Green knight! Ha, ha, ha, ha! " said the heroic figure, handing Arthur a business card. It too was green.

"Yes – you are, aren't you!" replied the king. He pulled a piece of stray door handle from his hair.

"And he can't… (cough) (cough)," coughed Guinevere. She would have continued, but her mouth was crammed with sawdust.

"What your not-green queen means to say is that I, the great Green Knight, can't be harmed by any man alive. Ha, ha, ha, ha!" added the Green Knight helpfully.

"Is that so?" asked Arthur, swinging his boot back and aiming at a spot just below the Green Knight's belt. He thought better of it and read the card some more.

Guinevere ventured to the window. "Time for some fresh air (cough). It's so dusty in here (cough), I can't stop coughing (cough)."

Arthur rose from what was left of the cupboard and greeted his visitor and saviour.

"Welcome Green Knight," said the king. "Your timing is perfect. Camelot needs the help of a brave and noble hero!"

"I know," replied the Green Knight with a green smile. "That's why you're paying me such a high price in gold!"

"We're what?!?!?" yelled Arthur in a rage. He shot a mean look at Guinevere who simply shrugged.

Looking at the king, it was hard to tell whether he was pleased or furious. He was glad of the help but rather cross about having to pay through the nose for the services of one green knight. Still, it was far cheaper than paying the Round Table's medical bills.

"Ha, ha, ha, ha! Have no fear, you king, you," laughed the expensive visitor. "I have not met a foe who could best in combat yet. With one swing of my mighty axe, your enemies will be little more than a pile of pots and pans. Ha, ha, ha, ha!"

"I'm sure you could beat them all up and be back in time for lunch," giggled Guinevere, playing the part of a welcoming hostess. "A big bulking hero like you probably needs a big bulky lunch. Well, you're in luck. We have the finest chefs in Britain."

"Ha, ha, ha, ha! Yum-Yum!" replied guess who.

"You're welcome to whatever my cat hasn't eaten," said the king.

"Pardon?" The Green Knight wanted to be sure years of battle hadn't made his ears faulty.

"Ignore my husband," said Guinevere, leading the green giant away by the elbow. She hadn't told the Green Knight about Sir Softpaws for many good reasons. "Why don't you get settled into your room? The servants are painting it green as we speak. You can meet the rest of the kingdom tomorrow."

The next day, all Camelot piled into the town square to see the enormous green visitor for themselves. He entertained peasant after peasant through amazing feats of strength. With one arm, he lifted a hundred townspeople piled on high. Next he threw a horse and cart clean over the mountains in a single throw. When he accidentally dropped his sword posing for a portrait. he caused a small earthquake. Finally, he dropkicked Clive the interior designer into a lake over a hundred miles away (Clive was from the letter earlier and Clive thought green was last season's colour).

Things were a little tense when Sir Softpaws magically appeared (many remembered his squishing of Lancelot). But the Green Knight was more than prepared to handle the carelessly curious cat. Thankfully, he kept a green ball of yarn ready for any situation. One toss of the bouncy woolen ball down the street and Softpaws took off after it. He was occupied for many hours and having a lot of fun trying to untangle himself. The crowd lapped all of this up and rolled out the welcome mat for their new green hero.

In the hospital, the lesser knights of Camelot were less impressed. They had to stay in bed and be in lots of pain. Rumour said they were particularly miffed when Arthur didn't invite them to the banquet in the Green Knight's honour later that evening. Instead the king just sent them one 'get well soon' card and a basket of half-eaten grapes.

Chapter 15
Anything The Cat Didn't Eat

Owing to the appetite of a monstrous cat, the banquet at Camelot was not as bountiful as previous feasts. They were short by about 300 cooked turkeys, 20 roasted pigs and 50 fat geese. Curiously, not a single freshwater tuna was to be found for miles. In fact, all the castle cooks had managed to prepare was a landslide of dried crackers with broccoli paste, a small plate of takeaway sandwiches and, to Arthur's surprise, endless plates of old plums and prunes which the cat didn't seem to care for.

"Again, I am so, so, so sorry about the food. Would you care for a fistful of prunes?" said Guinevere, "How about another cracker?" The court atmosphere matched the sad scraps of food being served. The musicians were underfed. Thus, there was no music, nor poems, no story of brave deeds. Only a plummy burp now and again interrupted the grumbling court.

"Thank you, but no, my lady. I have already eaten enough prunes and plums to feed a thousand vegan werewolves. Ha, ha, ha, ha!"

The Green Knight was in a merry mood. "It is said that on the eve of battle, even a seasoned warrior has to choose his food with care. Certain tasties can play havoc with his guts. For when the battle rages, he may ache for the use of a nearby loo..."

"Um, er. So have you been fighting anywhere interesting?" interrupted the king, in a brave attempt to steer the conversation away from the lack of battlefield toilets.

"Why, only last week, I was fighting up the snowy mountains up yonder..." said the knight.

"Where?" asked the queen.

"Yonder. A land near Far Away. Twenty leagues west of Nowhere," the knight explained. "Now, I have braved some terrible places in my time, the most awful of environments, in Yonder I had to survive on melting snow and treating myself to a passing polar bear."

"Really?" replied Arthur. "I once went camping and lost my tent. So I know exactly how you feel."

The knight frowned as he bit down on "dry prune sandwich" made of many dry crackers. He gobbled into the crumbly snack and the dust sent the queen into another coughing fit.

"Good (cough) grief!" coughed the queen. "Not (cough) again (cough)!"

Hearing the queen's coughing fit, the courtiers stopped eating. They had had enough prunes.

Because everyone was so gloomy and glum, the Green Knight sprang to his feet, and shouted out a big promise to any who heard.

"Ha, ha, ha, ha! People of Camelot, I pledge to you by my very green honour that once I have defeated these invaders – sometime in the next few days, give or take a Tuesday – we will celebrate with the biggest banquet you have ever seen! Plates will break with food! Your cups will rust with drink! Memories will be made. Toilets will break. Bowels will be shattered! Your doctors will retire! Ha, ha, ha, ha!"

"Isn't he wonderful?" crooned Arthur to Guinevere. "Green Knight, cheer us all up and show what you've got planned for my enemies? And don't spare the nasty details!"

At that, the Green Knight laughed like a fox in an unguarded chicken pen. He raised his great green axe and, in a flash of blinding green light, sliced right through the banquet hall table. With a heavy blow, the thing was cut in half. Then he swished his great weapon again and again until what remained was nothing more than floating snowflakes of sawdust. This made Guinevere's cough ten times worse.

"Yay!" clapped Arthur squealing with delight. "Guards! Fetch me quill and paper! There's some very naughty letters I wish to write."

"Sorry your royal highness but we're out of quills," said a young guard. "On account of your cat eating everything in the kingdom with feathers. From the pelican to the zingy chicken strip, there's not a feather left to make a quill."

"Rats!" yelled Arthur. "Well in that case, fetch me Merlin's spare wands. I'll use them as some sort of pointy writing sticks."

The guards went off to ransack Merlin's laboratory some more. Stealing everything the wizard owned had been a cheap source of therapy for the king.

"Oh no!" wailed Guinevere. "Don't provoke them. If we lose..."

"Ha, ha, ha, ha!" said a certain green fool. "Provoke them to your heart's content, Sire. I'll make mincemeat out of anyone who harms my new best friend, King Arthur."

Arthur's eyes twinkled at the word 'friend'. Camelot might not be doomed after all.

Chapter 16
The Green Knight Goes Green...er

Arthur woke up with a sore head but pockets full of hope. Last night after the banquet, he had really gone overboard. When his hungry courtiers had returned to their beds, the king and his green best friend had stayed up late. They toured the castle and played endless games of 'hide and seek'. And instead of writing one insulting note, Arthur had enough excitement running through him to write many letters. He sent a letter to every soldier in the enemy army. Throughout all hours of the night, the squires of Camelot were sent out time and again to deliver them. The king was having too much fun to care if they came back or not.

Feeling safe again, today Arthur had lots of important 'king business' to do around the kingdom. Skipping through the streets while eating his morning cereal, the king felt quite jolly. With the sun shining and the peasants smelling better than normal, Arthur knew it was going to be a good morning. For once this week, things seemed to be going his way.

"Morning peasants," he said to anyone he met (even a few horses). "What a wonderful day", "How's the family", "Have you lost weight?" "Good hay today?" Arthur stopped by Camelot Coffee and helped himself to a morning cup of brown.

At last, the king started on his chores for the day (Guinevere had given him a 'list' of odd jobs to do around town). He visited the Camelot fisherman, who were on strike because of Sir Softpaws. He went to the blacksmiths to see how much a king-sized suit of green armour would cost. He spent many hours in the town hall listening to peasants complain. He went to the Camelot kettlepot collectors to judge the best kept Camelot kettlepot. He opened a children's hospital and was promptly told off for running with the oversized novelty scissors. The crown jewels were polished and the thrones were cleaned. Then it was time to visit the bank, where not even the huge cost of renting one green knight and feeding one cat with a bottomless stomach couldn't bring the king down. Later, with chores complete. Arthur had some free time. He decided to take a trip to his private archery range.

Arthur was preparing to fire an arrow from his favourite bow when a man in a white coat ran onto court. He was careful to remove his boots and put on a pair of white trainers (that way he wouldn't scuff the court). The man looked like he had serious business. Arthur simply sighed. He aimed for the target but his shot landed in a nearby bush and bothered a small nest of sparrows.

"My lord!" wailed the man, dodging the king's next arrow. "You must come to the hospital at once." He was the Head Healer of Camelot Hospital.

"Oh, what could it possibly be now?!" grumped the king. "Can't I have a few minutes to myself?" Arthur had been having such a good day. That part of the day had now ended.

"Your knights, my lord," replied the Head Healer. "You promised you'd pay them a visit."

Arthur had meant to visit them, but, you know, stuff happened. He was a very busy king after all.

The very busy king shot another arrow (which somehow hit the bullseye on the wrong target).

The hospital was not a pretty sight. Arthur's poor knights were in pretty bad shape.

The king drifted past bed after bed. Each held an injured knight. He tried not to stare at the nastier wounds (of which there were many). A junior healer was removing nettles from Sir Bors's rear end while a gentle nurse applied ointment for very deep horse bites. Sir Headstrong was half his original height. Sir Percival had blisters all over his feet. Lancelot's lance was gently being removed from a delicate area belonging to Sir Gawain and Sir Bedivere had nothing more serious than a slight tickle in the throat. However he had a convincing doctor's note excusing him from armed combat until the next month. The rest were too gruesome to describe.

Arthur tried his best to cheer them up which was a bad idea. The king couldn't think of anything to say off the top of his head. He was a lousy singer and no good at small talk. He wanted to write a poem called 'Get well soon', but, if anything, poetry would only make his knights sicker. Instead,

Arthur chose to entertain them with tales about his new best friend, the Green Knight. Nobody wanted to hear it. So the king decided to be useful and helped himself to any uneaten grapes. Since Sir Tristan had his mouth wired shut, he wouldn't miss them.

Last of all, Arthur passed a bed containing most of Sir Lancelot. The king's former favourite had the worst injuries of them all. He was bruised and broken more than every knight put together. Not to mention flatter than the lot of them. Sir Softpaws had squashed him like a tinned tomato. So, bandaged from head to toe, for a Knight of the Round Table, he looked exactly like that: a round table.

"Hello Lancelot, how are those broken bones healing?" asked Arthur. Nodding sympathetically at his muffled answer, Arthur sneakily took back his Camelot Coffee gift card. He could use it as the grand prize for the next tournament.

The king continued. "I've talked with Sir Softpaws, when he wasn't signing autographs, and I think if he were here today, he'd want to tell you from the bottom of his kitty-cat heart how sorry he truly is."

"Mwupmh!" Lancelot wasn't convinced.

"He's not a bad cat really," Arthur continued. "He's just a little clumsy. I mean, if you were his size, I wouldn't be surprised if you squashed a couple of bystanders, even if you had four legs!"

Arthur laughed at this 'joke'. Lancelot "Mwumph-ed" in fury.

"Now, don't you worry about little old me, Lance-a-not-alot-now-but-maybe-in-the-future," said the king sitting on the bed. "I've already replaced you with a brand new greener-upgrade. He goes by the name of The Green Knight, but I'm trying to call him Ol' Greeny. Want to see a picture?"

Arthur was draining the last drops of conversation from the small talk barrel. The king might have yammered on further, but he was interrupted by the Head Healer.

"Please, sire. Follow me. There's more bad news."

The Head Healer led the king through the hospital hallway to a private room. With a bony finger, he pointed Arthur toward the bad news. He gulped with dread. Pushing open the door slowly and with his eyes closed, Arthur came face to face with disaster. There, lying in bed and making strange moaning noises was none other than the Green Knight. He looked really, really green now.

"Ol' Greeny!" wailed Arthur. "What happened to you?"

"Ha ha ha! UHHHHHHH!" groaned the knight, now extremely green.

"What is it, brave knight? Has someone cast an evil spell on you?"

"UHHHHHHHHHH!"

"Is it a horrid curse from some ill-willed magician?"

"UHHHHHHHHHH!"

"Is it homesickness?"asked the king, instantly regretting it. It was never homesickness.

"UHHHHHH!" replied the Green Knight holding his stomach. "Last night… the banquet... I... I shouldn't have had all those blasted plums and prunes. They are waging war in my tum-tum and everybody's losing." At that, he let out a gassy burp and the flowers on his bedside table melted.

"Come on, greeny. A few bits of mouldy old fruit shouldn't stop a big, strong warrior, like yourself. Am I right?" said Arthur. He hoped he was.

"Ha, ha, ha! Uh... uh… uh… uh-oh!" cried the green knight, letting out a volley of 'bottom burps' which we refuse to write about here.

Just then, Arthur heard a noise that sounded like ten crows in an argument. Somehow it sounded familiar. As the king rushed out into the hallway to investigate, he quickly realized what the noise was and where it was coming from. Arthur entered another private room near the back of the hospital and drew back the curtain. In bed, holding her stomach, was the queen.

"Oh no, Guinevere! Don't tell me you ate the prunes too?" he gasped.

"Don't talk to me ever again. Oooooo!" wailed the queasy queen. "Why did I ever let you talk me into holding a banquet?"

"Sorry, my dear." Arthur grovelled, kissing her hand for good measure. "How was I to know a prune and cracker banquet would make you so sick? I've seen you eat worse."

"Eat worse?!?!?!" Guinevere frowned like an unfed bulldog. "Get out! Out! Out!" she roared. Arthur fled the scene ducking underneath a flock of flying bedpans.

Chapter 17

Cheap Defenders in Straw Underpants

Over the next few days, Guinevere's guts were an active volcano and Arthur's mood was no better. Both grumbled in their own way. Both were slowly edging closer to being explosive. With nobody left to help him get off a mountain of trouble, the king was running low on back up plans. Somehow he had to save the day all by himself. Besides, he was fresh out of good hiding places.

What was worse, the enemy army had finally replied to Arthur's insults. The king's messengers had been sent back to Camelot covered in sticky tar and feathers. Each one had a letter painted on his chest so if they all stood in the correct order, the message spelled out: "Now It's Personal!" The king had accidentally read "Sit on Neal's Prow!" and had wasted the day down the shipyard looking for Captain Neal.

Arthur spent the next morning and much of that afternoon in front of the castle walls digging a massive trench (which he had a great deal of trouble escaping later). Playing in the mud, the king had time to think. He remembered a famous battle plan used by another king from a faraway land. Like Arthur, this king too did not have enough knights to defend his castle. So, using his imagination, this king had created a fake army to frighten away his enemies. Arthur's imagination was lousy so he just copied the faraway king's idea instead.

"Amazing!" cried Arthur – to no one in particular. At least he had escaped the trench. With a brand new energy, the king got to work and collected every spare weapon and piece of armour he could find (the best came from the Camelot gift shop). Leaving these shiny things in a shiny pile outside the castle walls, Arthur was able to swipe some unused sacks from the Camelot mill. Then he chatted to the Guild of Old Lady Knitters over tea and biscuits and took a couple of reams of yarn for tying things up. Only then did Arthur's plan go sideways – he couldn't find any straw (and had a terrible relationship with Camelot's farmers).

"Stuff it!" the king cried, almost giving up on this task then and there.

The king wandered around town as he gazed sadly at the floor. Today was market day. He caught sight of a row of carts parked outside the Cobblestone Inn (nicknamed "The Crown and Twit" after the king himself). The first cart was full of dusty bricks. The second cart was full of brown goo. The third cart was filled with (if the royal eyes were not mistaken) something yellow and pokey that wasn't bananas.

"Straw!" declared Arthur with joy. He skipped along the street in excitement.

Arthur's spirits rose as he strode briskly across the market square to talk to the carts' owner. Approaching the unguarded vehicles, his spirits sank. They bore the name "T.Cotter and Sons."

"Stuff it!" said the king... again. Terry Cotter was the richest man in Camelot. He was well known for ripping off good folk with his high prices and low quality workmanship. His newest con bore the name 'T. Cotter and Sons' but everyone knew Cotter's sons were so sick of their wheeler-dealer dad that they'd run off to join a travelling flea circus. The same dad was leaving the inn now, smelling faintly of chicken and leek pie.

"Cotter, my good man!" Arthur approached Terry with a broad grin, trying to sound as if he often talked to common folk. "How are things in... whatever it is you do?"

Terry Cotter's face was as blank as a barn wall, but his eyebrows cocked at the thought of money. It was an impressive instinct often seen in hungry wolves. Terry did much business with rich folk throughout many kingdoms. So he knew full well when they were trying to suck up to him and when something was going down. And when something was going down, his prices went up.

"What can I do for your Royal Highness?" he asked, standing still and silent as he waited for the king to reply.

"What do you say to being a good fellow and selling that cart load of straw over here?" said Arthur trying to be cute. "It's for a friend of mine. Big into chewing straw he is. Good for the gums and all that."

The merchant smiled but did not move.

"Or would you believe me if I said it was for the sick

children of Camelot." The king grit his knuckles and tried to produce a tear. He almost fainted. "They need all the food they can get. Bread is so expensive these days. Straw is just as good. For the growing boys and girls." The king's face was red with effort, but his eyes were dry as the straw he was trying to get.

Still, Terry Cotter stood there and didn't say a word.

"Fine!" snapped Arthur. "I need straw. For stuffing my model army." He continued to bluster. "You have a whole cartful of straw over there. So bring it here. I haven't got all day!"

"It'll cost you," said the crafty merchant.

"How much?" asked the king. Of course, he was not going to get anything from Cotter for free.

"Twenty," said the merchant flatly.

"T-t-t-twenty silver coins for a few bags of straw?" stammered the King in a rage.

"Gold coins," corrected Cotter.

"That's daylight robbery!" moaned the king.

"Price's are skyrocketing," said Terry without batting an eyelid. "There's a straw shortage, you see."

"Straw shortage?" cried Arthur.

"Yes, sire. In case you haven't heard, there's a war on," said Cotter pretending to be offended. "Your war I believe. Also, thanks to that cat of yours needing a litter tray the size of a farmer's field, I can't just give this away, can I?"

Arthur blustered, but he had no other choices. Twenty golden coins were handed over in a crotchety grunt.

Outside the castle walls, Arthur got back to his stuffing. After many long hours of stuffing stuff into other stuff, he had crafted a full scarecrow army of dummy knights. From far away, the fake knights looked rather frightening. Their armour was polished. Their swords were pointy. The king (who had never been good at art) was over the moon with his new soldiers. But he had worked very hard today. He deserved an afternoon nap. So Arthur went out of the trench and nipped off to this bedroom for a kingly snooze.

This snooze soon turned into a short nap which turned into forty winks which turned into an almighty beauty sleep with full-blown snoring. For, while Arthur slept soundly, his scarecrow army quickly became a must-see tourist attraction.

In no time at all, peasants and their families were queuing up around the castle walls to get their portraits painted next to the strange new figures. Thanks to his nose for business, Terry Cotter had set up a ticket booth and, in no time at all too, he was charging money to see them.

The "Terry Cotter army" (since Terry had named them after himself) was a smash hit and had soon made the man a tidy sum. T-shirt sales alone were ridiculous. If the faraway king (whose idea it was) had been a man of business, he would have been proud. However, word of "Terry Cotter's army" must have reached Arthur's enemy, because when Arthur returned to the ramparts later that day, he found his beautiful straw-filled soldiers ripped to pieces. All the armour and weapons had been stolen too. Nothing had been left behind except a message. It read:

Dear Arthur (King),

Thanks for the free stuff. You're too generous a stinker.

Sincerely

Your enemies.

"Why do I keep reading their letters?" Arthur thought to himself. "Nothing good ever comes from reading them." With all the humbug going down in Camelot, the king couldn't be too mad. These foes may be deadly and out to destroy him, but at least they took the time to write proper letters. The penwork was superb. Despite their contents, good handwriting was its own reward.

Chapter 18
A King Sulks From on High

Arthur sulked as he sat on the castle battlements. His little legs dangled over the walls high above a great drop. To pass the time, he flicked pebbles over the wall's edge and waited for the sound of a satisfying splash from the moat below. The last three had landed on the heads of three enemy scouts on patrol and annoyed them greatly. But this brought the king no comfort. Not only was he aiming for somewhere else, but every time he tried to solve the problems facing his kingdom, he had only made them worse.

As a young king, Arthur thought he was rather good in a crisis. Just by yanking a two-handed broadsword from some rock, he had brought peace to Camelot. That worked out quite well. Then he sent his knights all over Britain to do something heroic or other. Soon, he had rid the nutberry wood of poisonous squirrels by introducing poisonous owls. He signed a peace treaty with the Fruit trolls and promised never to eat an apricot ever again. He even sorted out the parking problem outside Camelot Bakery by feeding the traffic wardens nothing but cupcakes.

Arthur began to think about his career as a king since then, and the thought failed to bring him comfort. His best deeds had been accomplished with the help of his faithful magician Merlin. The wizard was a talented pencil pusher and never stole more than five percent per year. Where was that confounded wizard when you needed him? Merlin had been gone for weeks.

By now, the king had run out of pebbles and so moved onto roof tiles. As he flung the next tile over the wall, Arthur was puzzled to watch it stop in mid-air and gently float back to its starting place. The battlements were then instantly cleaned and the wall completely repaired. They had also been repainted with fish and birds as if by magic.

"Meow?" came a deep voice from behind him. It appeared out of nowhere. The hulking figure sat down with an ear-splitting crunch. The magic of Sir Softpaws truly knew no bounds.

"Oh, hello, Sir Softpaws. Have you got bored of playing with the villagers?" sighed Arthur. Something in his voice suggested he was at the point of resigning as king and setting up his own turnip farm in a land far away.

"Meow," shrugged Softpaws. He crouched on the wall and began to laze about. He stretched out a leg to have a scratch and accidentally drop-kicked a turret clean over the horizon.

"I know how you feel," said Arthur "I too have an itch, the itch of being sad. And I need a happy scratch to make it better."

The cat sensed his owner was feeling blue. So he nuzzled Arthur with his gigantic head covering the king in enough ginger fur to make an excellent winter coat.

"I know, I know," mused the king as he pulled off lumps of fur. "Things haven't been going well for me lately. Nothing I do seems to help. Oh Softpaws, what are we going to do?"

The cat placed an affectionate paw on his owner's shoulders (this time careful not to squash anything). Something in the cat's eyes said 'everything's going to be OK' or 'you forgot to feed me.' Arthur had trouble reading emotions on human faces, let alone the triangle faces of cats.

The pair sat together on the battlements and watched the setting sun. The stone ramparts overlooked the beautiful green fields around Camelot. They stretched on for miles as far as the eye could see. Only a well-worn country path or sometimes a farmer's cottage broke up the never-ending meadows of grass and grain. It was such a lovely view, thought Arthur, no wonder the price of houses, huts and hovels were skyrocketing. Somewhere out there, hordes of steel-clad invaders were marching on Camelot with swords in hand and hearts full of hate. Arthur sighed and Sir Softpaws purred loudly and, having found the ability to shoot lasers from his eyes, blasted a passing seagull to deep-fried singe.

"Clever boy!" said Arthur, patting the furry wall that was his cat. "When did you learn to do that?"

Sir Softpaws made no answer. His tummy rumbled and clearly said 'beware' in Italian. Arthur didn't mind. The magic mog was certainly useful. Together, king and cat dined on roast seagull, which Softpaws had cooked evenly and to a crisp.

Halfway through tucking into a seagull drumstick, Arthur had an idea. He looked lovingly at his pet. The giant cat was his last hope and prayer. Maybe there was still a reason not to throw in the royal towel just yet.

"Sir Softpaws! You beautiful big dangerous boy! Why don't you defend Camelot for me?"

"Meow?" mewed Sir Softpaws. He looked puzzled.

"Of course, you can," said Arthur. "Look what you did to Lancelot. He put all my knights in hospital and you splattered him like a tinned tomato. Now with Merlin gone, Guinevere not talking to me, and Ol' Greeny sick in bed with the pruney splatters, you are Camelot's most dangerous warrior!"

"Meow?" the cat replied. He didn't speak English.

"OK, OK." Arthur thought for a second. "So you haven't had any training, but with your fireballs, laser eyes and anything else you're hiding from me." The cat gave a confused look. " I'm sure you can skip a couple of classes."

Arthur gave Sir Softpaws a big hug. The cat let out a purr that caused lightning to shoot down from the sky. It missed Arthur by inches.

"And I shall be the one who trains you!" shouted an overjoyed Arthur. He ran a hand through his hair making sure he wasn't on fire. Sir Softpaws merely shrugged. Whoever won the coming war would have to feed him anyhow.

Chapter 19
The Training of Sir Softpaws

Training a cat is easier said than done. Any pet store owner or lion tamer will tell you that. Cats like to sleep. Cats need lots of fish before they even try. They get easily distracted. They don't follow instructions. They have contempt for anyone teaching them new tricks. The next morning, Arthur woke up bright and early to give it a try. Rumours had spread around Camelot of what he had in mind, so everyone else also woke up bright and early to laugh at him.

Arthur had set up training dummies around the jousting stadium (it hadn't been used once since the last tournament and locals believe the place was cursed). The dummies were dressed like enemy generals and the king had scribbled a very angry look on their faces. Ever since building the 'Terry Cotter army' single-handedly, Arthur had finally found a hobby he liked – arts and crafts. In the future, he would spend many hours building dummies of people he didn't like. But now was not the time for hobbies. Now was the dawn of the world's first warrior cat.

With Sir Softpaws by his side, Arthur pointed Excalibur toward the dummy and with a bold cry, called out his orders. "Attack Softpaws! Show no mercy! Heart of a lion! Speed of a cheetah!"

Letting out a fierce growl, Sir Softpaws charged towards his target. The ground shook as he ran at full speed. The dummy had no chance. But, instead of chewing its head off like he was told, the cat began to cuddle the dummy and gave it a gentle lick. He may be the size of a tank, but Softpaws didn't yet have the cold heart of a knight.

A mildly annoyed Arthur marched up to the dummy. "Not like that, Sir Softpaws – like this!"

The king swung Excalibur wildly at the dummy, missed its head by at least a metre, and watched helplessly as his sword flew from his hand. The would-be battle-cat looked at him, confused. If Softpaws could ask them, he had questions.

"Like that! But a little lower," explained the king, blushing as he picked Excalibur from the grass. The crowd who had gathered to watch Sir Softpaws's training hooted and hollered to their hearts' content. At least, they were having a good time.

Next on Arthur's training programme was archery. Now, most knights are a bit sniffy about archers. The bow and arrow is hardly a very noble weapon. You can hide behind a tree or a rock and shoot arrows at people without being brave enough to look them in the eye (which is why it was Arthur's favourite weapon. With a big enough bow, he didn't even have to leave the castle). However, the king knew his student was big and shaky on his legs. In close combat, he was just as likely to squish friend as he was foe. For this reason, archery was Sir Softpaws's next lesson.

Unfortunately, like all cats, Softpaws didn't have any thumbs – which made holding arrows difficult. So the cat was taught how to use a catapult instead. At first, this went rather well. Sir Softpaws quickly figured out how to press the button that made the big boulder shoot in the air (Arthur had painted a 'paw' on the button to give the cat a clue). Unfortunately, Sir Softpaws wasn't a very good aim. After a few rocks landed in downtown Camelot, one stray missile landed in the town's duck pond and soaked the crowd of onlookers. This time, Arthur hooted and hollered. At least, he was having a good time.

Next, Arthur tried teaching Sir Softpaws how to sneak up on unsuspecting enemies. Cats are, of course, known for their stealth. They can stay perfectly still waiting outside a mousehole without moving a whisker. Or they can pad silently through a garden at night after spending the day at a neighbour's house. Or, while you're sleeping, they can creep up onto your bed and sit on your face. They are perfect ninjas.

But, in the case of Sir Softpaws, sneaking up on things was impossible. This is what Arthur learned when he played "Red light/Green light" with his cat. As the king leant against a tree with his eyes closed, Softpaws crept slowly towards him. The cat kept his balance and paused like a statue whenever Arthur turned around. Alas, he was so enormous that the ground quaked whenever he moved a paw. No enemy would ever believe he wasn't there. Plus, toward the end of the lesson, the cat had tried to climb the tree (cats like doing this). Now there was no tree.

So what was the answer? Arthur thought. Sir Softpaws was too meek to be a warrior cat. He was a rotten shot. He was far too noisy to sneak up on anything that didn't have its ears stuffed with cheese. Arthur decided to put an end to the training and pretend the cat passed his tests with flying colours. With his endless magical powers, Softpaws could afford to skip a class or two. Besides, the cat could just sit on anything that displeased him. This was the best tactic Arthur had come up with so far. "Cat's bum: one. Enemy: nill!" Arthur chuckled. "When in doubt, do what you do best!"

The best blacksmiths in Camelot were summoned. They tried and failed to forge a weapon big enough for Sir Softpaws to use. No fire would be large enough to melt the metal they needed. No sword would be sharper than his kitty claws. The king's warrior cat would simply have to go into battle 'unarmed'. He would have to defend himself using nothing but fireballs, laser eyes, lightning storms, teleporting, and anything else that came to mind.

At least the blacksmiths had a bit of success. They were able to assemble something that came close to a suit of armour for the cat. For his breastplate, they glued together three cottages each with a straw roof (for added comfort). To protect his legs, four chimneys were found. Finally, his head was protected by a helmet made from an upturned boat (the S.S. Honeybun) which fitted snugly over his fluffy ears. Dressed in armour and with his lessons learnt, Sir Softpaws had officially completed his 'training'. Now it was time for him to be officially knighted.

Chapter 20
Arise... Sir Softpaws

Although they certainly weren't invited, every lord, lout, clod, churchman, peasant, big wig, plonker, and crook in Camelot had barged their way into Arthur's throne room. They were all here to see Sir Softpaws be knighted. As always, they were still his biggest fans (even though many were dripping wet from the catapult incident earlier).

There wasn't enough room for Sir Softpaws in the throne room. Instead, the cat sat outside and poked his face through an open window twelve floors up. He seemed flattered by the attention. Arthur wondered if he ever missed the perks of being an inside cat, like thick carpets and a warm fireplace.

With the help of a stepladder, Arthur dabbed his sword onto the bulky shoulders of his cat. Since most knights had much less fur over their face and body, the king was extra careful not to give Softpaws an unwanted haircut. One sword tap, two taps later. The king proclaimed the knight of the Round Table's oath (which Arthur had written himself).

"Sir Softpaws, I hereby dub you a Knight of the Round Table. You are Camelot's sword and shield and must do absolutely anything I tell you. I am king. That is important. You must do what I say, no questions asked, and you must look good doing it. From this day forward you are no longer Sir Softpaws," he paused. "Arise... Sir Sir Softpaws."

The crowd burst into cheers and applause. Finally the kingdom's favourite cat had earned a 'sir' in his name (His soft paws were never up for debate).

"Hooray, Sir Sir Softpaws!" They cheered. "Hooray! Hooray! Hooray for Sir Sir Softpaws!" The cat blushed. It had been almost an hour since he had last been praised.

"And what about three cheers for his owner, the king!" chirped Arthur. "Let's not forget the ruler who had the good sense to train his cat into such a fearsome weapon. Without me, Camelot would be doomed. Three cheers for King Arthur the problem-solver!"

The king's words were met with stone cold silence. Most people felt a bit embarrassed on their ruler's behalf. A few folks on the front row tried to stroke the cat. He welcomed their affection. Someone had even brought him a fish tank full of milk. But soon Softpaws was distracted by a fluttering flag and began to play with it instead.

Arthur fumed at this insult. "Well, if you like Sir Softpaws so much, why don't you go ahead and make the cat your king?

"We can do that?" whispered a woman at the front. She was pleasantly surprised.

"Good idea!" called a voice from the back. Everyone began to mutter similar words.

"Anyone would be better than that fool, Arthur!' said a voice that sounded like Terry Cotter.

"Good idea!" they yelled. "All hail King Sir–"

"I was only kidding!" wailed Arthur. He was rightfully worried. Camelot had so few popular public figures. Arthur hadn't been one since he pulled the sword from the stone. "Bring on the music!" he ordered, keen to change the subject.

To celebrate the special occasion, a court minstrel entered holding a golden harp and a bundle of sheet music. It was tradition that every knight on being knighted received a free song about himself. Previous belters included "Lancelot: he loves to lance a lot", "Gawain is the word", and "The best you ever Galahad". This one was called 'The Ballad of Sir Softpaws' which is sung throughout the kingdom to this day (despite long being since banned by royal command). And it went like this:

Oh, who's the cutesy-wootsy moggy we adore?
Softpaws Softpaws, the kitty knight of lore.
His fluffy tail and button nose, give us all a grin
Softpaws, Softpaws, everyone loves him!

So hear him mew. Meow! Meow!
And hear him purr. Wow! Wow!
The Britons know there is one thing
Be ye man or mouse or horse
In Camelot the people sing
Softpaws rules of course!

The hall erupted with cheers and everyone sang the words again and again and again. It had a catchy rhythm, and was considered by everyone to be a real toe-tapper. Everyone, except Arthur. He felt the last verse didn't portray him in the best light.

"I order you to quiet down! Song's over!" yelled the king. He was jealous of the fuss people were making. "I'm your king and protector! Don't forget whose face is on the money." Arthur stamped his right royal foot so hard his chainmail rattled.

"Sir Softpaws is the only protection we need!" said one.

"Yeah. And I think he'd look great on the money!" added another.

"But- but- but... he can't even hold a sword!" stuttered the jealous king.

"Neither can you!" called Terry Cotter from the back. The whole room exploded into chuckles.

By now, Sir Sir Softpaws was gone. He got bored and left a long time ago. This allowed a soothing breeze to come through the window which did nothing to cool the king's anger.

"But I'm saving Camelot!" whined Arthur, stamping this time with the left royal foot (he'd hurt his right royal right stamping it moments ago).

"Prove it!" said a cheeky peasant who the king couldn't make out from the crowd.

"Yeah! Prove it!" said an equally cheeky peasant.

"Very well, I shall," boasted Arthur. "Tomorrow, it will be I who leads a heroic charge and none other. Sir Softpaws will follow behind me, keeping well away from the 'hero zone'. The enemy army won't know what hit them!" There was a stunned hush over the audience. Arthur couldn't believe he said that either.

"I'll believe it when I see it," grumbled Terry Cotter. He helped himself to a glass of milk and sat on the window ledge.

"You will, Cotter," shot back Arthur. "You will." The king was getting tired of him so he slumped down in his throne and began to sulk.

"I'm sure I will," scoffed Cotter. "By the way, they're here."

"Who's there?"

"Them, your highness." With a grin, Terry Cotter pointed out the window. Many from the crowd rushed over and looked outside. All together, they gasped in shock.

"It's the enemy! The enemy is here!" they cried. "We're surrounded. There's so many of them!"

A grim panic gripped Arthur. He tried to sneak a peek but too many people were blocking the window. He hopped up and down hoping to see above them, but they were too tall. Thinking on his feet, the king rushed out the throne room, ran through the royal corridors and, opening the back door, climbed up the stone steps to the castle roof. In no time at all, Arthur could see everything from the highest point in the kingdom.

Sure enough, there was the entire enemy army in their millions. They covered the fields of Camelot like countless ants at a hundred picnics (this was especially true since a few were helping themselves to the local farmers' crops. After all, they had marched many miles to get here). For now, the enemy army mostly waited patiently outside the castle walls while goblins and smaller soldiers began to build their camps.

"Rats!" said Arthur. "Where's my cat gone?" Cupping his hands around his mouth he began to call Sir Softpaws as if he were late to dinner. "Here Sir Softpaws! Here Sir Softpaws! Here kitty kitty kitty! Come out and save my kingdom!"

Chapter 21
Your Doom is Here, King Arthur

The day was finally here, the day Arthur had been dreading. The king had tried lots of ways to delay them: turning all of the road signs the wrong way; bribing local shepherds to give wrong directions; and when all else failed, moving every hedge, shrub and country wall in the kingdom so they no longer matched the maps. Sadly he only succeeded in confusing a lot of sheep. Filling Camelot's fields with countless grim-faced soldiers, it looked like the enemy army was here to stay – and what an army it was...

On their long march to Camelot, the gang of kings had recruited many fearsome allies. They came from all four corners of the British Isles (including an extra bit called "Cornwall") and numbered no less than many, many, a lot of much. Endless rows of soldiers were clad in black armour and held pointy and scary this and that. Squads of enemy knights galloped on their mighty steeds, looking for trouble and leaving trails of horse mess behind them. Following this came troops of ghouls, goblins, giant lizards, griffins, and gollums all under the command of trustworthy vampires.

From the castle walls, Arthur could see four teams of trolls for hire and quite a lot of pixies who he had personally cheated out of money. There was even the odd young dragon who'd come out for some work experience. Among them were witches, wizards and wayward wish granters operating cauldrons and catapults and cannons. Not forgetting the swarms of mean-looking archers and stone slingers bringing up the rear. Many had nothing better to do and were itching for excitement.

"Arthur!" shouted a voice. The shout was accompanied by the heavy clunking from a suit of armour designed for the modern woman. The king turned to see who called. It was Guinevere and she had recovered from her tummy troubles (we hope).

"Guinevere, you're back!" said Arthur, stating the obvious.

"I'm well. Thanks for asking," snorted the queen.

"How is Ol' Greeney? Did he get my card?" Arthur never knew when to shut up.

The queen looked out at the enemy army below. Her face was full of concern. "Are you sure it's wise to leave the job of protecting Camelot to a cat?" she asked. "I've never seen him so much as pounce on a mouse and there are some pretty scary enemies out there. Have you thought about just saying sorry?"

"Ha!" snorted Arthur. "True, Sir Softpaws used to be a gentle soul back only a few hours ago. But, in one afternoon, I have transformed him into the four legged warrior of doom."

"Really?" said the queen. "One afternoon, huh?"

"Yes. He laughs in the face of danger like it had cornflakes stuck to its cheeks."

"That's good," The queen picked at her nails. "Because I think I saw a few fiery red dragons out there today. A bunch of trolls with big clubs too. All were pretty scary. Do you think the cat would mind going out and laughing in their face a little?"

"Meow! Meow! Meow!" meowed Softpaws. With a raised paw, he pointed at Arthur who had accidentally tucked his armour into his teddy bear underwear. Whether it was a laugh or not is best left to your imagination. Either way the cat returned to licking himself shortly after.

"See?" said Arthur. "He was laughing in your face just then!"

"Well, don't come crying to me when this goes wrong," said Guieneve seriously. With that she huffed off in a strop.

"We'll show her, won't we?" said Arthur. But there was no 'meow' in agreement. "Softpaws? Softpaws?"

Arthur turned to Sir Softpaws, but the cat pulled a face like he was sucking on a very sour grape. In fact, he began to look a little sick. He'd stopped licking his paws and started to cough.

"Softpaws? Are you alright?" asked Arthur, hoping the answer was "yes" or at least "meow" with a positive nod. But the cat had stopped coughing and had now moved onto heavy wheezing. Then he went cross-eyed before making a noise somewhere between a burp and a whistle.

Lifting himself up by his back paws and bowing his head low, Sir Softpaws suddenly began to heave. He was quaking, and shaking, and belly-aching. Finally, he made a violent gasping noise from the pit of his stomach which sounded like "Uuuurrrrrgggcchhhh! Ugh! Rughch! Blugh!"

Arthur stared at him blankly. Slowly, the king realized this wasn't some sort of feline war cry. He was very disappointed.

"What's the matter, Softpaws?" said Arthur with one last hope for that war cry. "Spit it out!"

So, the poorly mog obeyed his king's order (though not in the way he might have liked). Sir Softpaws belched out the biggest hairball that Arthur had ever seen. It flew at least a hundred feet in the air, spun around, and landed with an almighty splat at the king's feet.

"Better out than in!" Arthur said with a grin. "I must say, cat, not one of your best magic spells. Better cut down on the hairballs and stick with the fireballs."

There was no meow in reply.

"Well, now that's behind us," continued the king, "time to charge through the gate and send my enemies packing! They'll regret the day they ever crossed the king and his battle-cat. Charge!"

Arthur waited for the would-be warrior to spring into action, but no springing actually happened.

"Let's try that again," muttered the king. "Go and get the enemy, cat! Charge!"

But still no springing into action happened again.

Arthur sank to the ground with his head in his hands and let out a stream of frustrated curses.

"Why doesn't ANYONE do what I say!!!" he screamed. "Why? Why? Why?!!!"

Suddenly there was a strange whiff of magic in the air. Arthur sniffed and opened his eyes.

There was Sir Softpaws, but no longer bigger than a house. No longer a soft-hearted giant. No longer likely to cause doom and destruction just by sitting on things. In fact, Sir Softpaws was back to his normal size, give or take a few pounds.

As usual, Arthur's plans were in ruins. He started to panic, also as usual.

"No, no, no, no, no, no," he yammered, "You can't turn

back to normal. Not now. No, I need you for, for..." He picked up the unfortunate cat and shook him like a ketchup bottle when there was no ketchup left. But the worst was true, Sir Softpaws was no longer magic. He purred sweetly, mightily relieved, and let out a cute little kitty hiccup.

A muffled cough came from the hairball, then a splutter, followed by some very rude words. It seemed the hairball was coughing up its very own hairball.

"Strange way for a magic hairball to behave," thought Arthur as he pinched his nose shut. "Wait. How should a magical hairball behave? What in the name of Excalibur is going on here?"

The ugly blob wobbled, shook, and fell apart into chunks of fishy smelling muck and stinky gooey cat fluff. From the mess emerged a strange figure covered in bits of globs. He wobbled to his feet. His pointed hat was all dented out of shape and his white beard had developed a grubby yellow tinge. His wand was covered in fish guts and the less said about his long wizard robes the better. He brushed himself down and began to speak.

"Hello, Arthur. Long time no see!" he said. "Um. You're probably wondering what happened to me. Well, it's a long story..."

Arthur strained and rubbed at his eyes trying to make out who the sticky figure was. At long last, two and two made four, standing before him and smelling like a wet fishmonger was none other than Merlin.

Chapter 22

Doomsday Dumbsday

"Merlin! Is it really you?" cried Arthur.

Yes, sire. It is I," said Merlin.

The king rushed toward his old mentor with arms wide open and wrapped his hands tightly around the wizard's throat. It was a gesture Arthur later swore had been a very special kind of hug.

"You're choking me!" Merlin wheezed. The wizard began to chant a magical spell and with a swing of his wrist, Arthur was flipped upside down and dangled in the air by some magical aura. With his feet on the ground, the king was frowning furiously, but at least it looked like he was smiling when he was upside down.

"You'd better have a good reason for leaving us in the lurch!" called Arthur, swinging his little legs in fury. "Also, I demand that you turn me the right way up this instant!"

"Is that any way to talk to an old friend?" said the wizard. "I've been inside your cat for the past three weeks, surviving on whatever he ate, which turns out was rather a lot."

Merlin patted his stomach for emphasis. The wizard had put on weight.

"What, how...?" demanded Arthur in angry amazement.

"Well it went like this..." said the wizard, magicking up a grainy flashback. "There I was, late at night in my tower. I was working on a recipe for a special chocolate milkshake that made you want to drink even more milkshakes. It was my latest gift to all of mankind. I was using only the best ingredients: chocolate, bubbles, eye of newt, worm's tongue, asbestos, and, of course, good old fashioned milk and cream. When I went out to the kitchen to fetch my magic sparkles, what did I return to find? Your confounded cat was lapping up my milkshake! I tried to shoo him away but when the furry thief tried to scurry away, he knocked over more than enough of my potions. There was a bing, a bang and a boom. All of a sudden, I was face to face with the mug of an enormous mog.

"And then he ate you? " said Arthur, knotting his eyebrows in doubt. "Hmm. I must admit, Merlin, this seems a little bit out of his kitty character."

"No, no, no, nothing like that," replied Merlin. "The cat didn't mean to eat me. Unfortunately, there was a lot of spilled milk on the floor and I, uh, well I sort of, well, you know… I, uh… slipped and, uh, was sort of, accidentally… swallowed."

"What a fascinating story. Could only happen to you." Arthur shrugged. He had bigger problems.

"Have no fear, Arthur! If a giant cat is what my king wants, a giant cat is what my king gets," boasted Merlin. "I can repeat the experiment no problemo. One quick trip down the shops to buy some chocolate and everything will be back to norm– WHAT IN THE NAME OF SORCERY IS THAT?!?!?!?!"

Merlin had just seen the massive army surrounding the castle. He began to panic while Arthur was cool as a cucumber (the king had gotten used to life-threatening danger by now).

"Sire, you should summon every knight in the kingdom--"

"Can't. Hospital," said the king,

"Then what about--"

"Can't. Out of money."

"Surely, you could--"

"Can't. No more food."

"Or what if--"

"Can't. No friends."

"But–"

"We're not on speaking terms."

"Then what in seven stars are you going to do?" said Merlin. "I spend a few weeks inside a cat and Camelot goes down the chamber pot. We're about to be toast!"

Arthur's attention returned to Sir Softpaws. He picked up the cat by his front haunches and looked at him for any evidence of leftover magic. Like all cats, when Softpaws was picked up by his front legs, he slowly started to sag like wet dough. It was not very magical, but it was quite cute.

"Come on Softpaws! You must have a little bit of magic power left. Anything? Maybe a little fireball? Can't you cough up one little fireball to save your king?" asked Arthur in a kind voice. He leaned in desperately looking down the cat's throat for any hint of magic that could pull them out of this dire situation. Sir Softpaws merely smiled and let out a fishy burp. Except for his stubby dragon tail, he was returned to being a pampered house cat once again.

"So much for that!" groaned Arthur, being licked by the cat for emphasis. "I guess it's time to go home and try again without the help of a magical monster cat. Back to the drawing board."

"I have the fullest confidence in you, my liege," said Merlin, drafting a letter of surrender. "I've just got to post something first."

Chapter 23
Plan B. Plan C. Plan D and a Half

Arthur was desperate. Sitting in his throne room, he slumped down into his seat further and further until his crown slipped from his forehead and rested over his eyes. Guinevere sat in the throne beside him weighing up which was better; being surrounded by many blood-hungry warriors or being sick in bed after eating the worst broccoli, plum and prune cocktail ever recorded (it was close).

Sir Softpaws padded in, finally able to fit through the catflap once more. He plopped himself on Guinevere's lap, purring happily and snorted a tiny pink bubble which popped. That was the last magical thing he ever did.

"Is there any better than a cat sitting on your lap," sighed Guinevere, feeding him a tasty treat from a silver bowl. "It's almost enough to forget the sheer horror that has been my intestines."

Arthur moaned. "Just when I needed a ferocious magical monster who can tackle trolls, destroy dragons and strike fear into the hearts of my enemies..." he said. "Out plops Merlin to ruin all my plans. It's time we faced facts. We're finished! The end is here!"

Sir Softpaws raised his head and gave him a nervous look. One of the side effects of Merlin's spell was that he had a slightly better grasp of the English language.

"Now, look at what you've done. You've upset our little boy!" said Gwinny in a silly voice that she reserved for babies and cats. "Don't listen to the nasty king Sir Softie!"

"I'm sorry, Softpaws!" sighed Arthur apologetically. No creature deserved to be talked to in a stupid voice like that.

"Yes, my pretty kitty," continued Guinevere. "Just ignore the silly, silly king. He's such a silly king, isn't he? A total wally. He's a very bad king… WHO HAS DOOMED CAMELOT!!! The silly voice had stopped. Guinevere frowned.

"What do you want me to do, Gwinny?" yelped the king . "I've gone through plans A and B and D and E. Even plan C for cat!" Arthur pointed at Softpaws. This time Sir Softpaws frowned. "I'm all out of ideas!"

"I've said it once and I'll say it again – apologize!" barked the queen. "Maybe they will all forget about your birthday fiasco like Captain Funnynuggets did."

"Captain Funnynuggets didn't forget. I paid him off with a bag of gold and sent him on a free trout tickling holiday," said Arthur. "That's not going to work with this enemy. I don't have any gold left. Besides, it wouldn't be fair on the trout."

"I could have a word with them. Maybe smooth things over?"

"You would? Arthur beamed.

"Of course, nobody's gone to war against me." Guinevere pointed to herself with pride. "Out of both of us, I'm the popular royal."

But just then, they were interrupted by another visitor. It appeared as blue, glowing smoke and got stuck halfway through the cat flap. After much grunting, it managed to squeeze through and take human form.

"Hey king. Catch!" Merlin threw Arthur a jar of sparkling purple liquid. Arthur fumbled the catch and watched it smash on the stone floor splashing purple liquid all over his feet. Then there was a hissing noise and the royal shoes seemed to dissolve to nothing and vanish into thin air, leaving nothing behind Arthur's naked toes and a faint smell of strawberries.

"Like it?" asked Merlin, grinning from ear to ear. He hoped they had forgotten about his botched entrance.

Arthur looked puzzled and more than a little worried.

"What is this? A magic shoe remover?" stammered the king. But then something incredible happened. His whole foot had disappeared. Then the other one. Nothing could be seen of the king's legs. Not his knobbly knees. Not even his razor-sharp toenails.

"Nope!" said Merlin. "Although that's not a bad idea. Could make a pretty penny. Magic shoe remover. I'd better write that down." The wizard pulled an enchanted feather from his pocket and muttered a few words. The quill flew through the air, found the nearest ink pot and flew back to jot down his latest get-rich scheme.

"Then in the name of trousers, what is it? Come on wizard!

Out with it!" cried the king in a mini rage because his legs were 'missing'.

"Sire, may I present the answer to all your problems… an invisibility potion!" declared Merlin. He looked very pleased with himself. Arthur pawed at where his feet used to be. Sure enough, they were still there. He nipped his finger on a toe nail.

"Now, I understand," said the king, sucking his pinky. "We will make my cat invisible, send him out alone into the enemy camp, and hope everyone has cat allergies."

"Not my first plan, sire," began Merlin. "Still I suppose I could..."

But Sir Softpaws did not like the direction this talk was going. He sprang up from Guinevere's lap and shot through the catflap faster than a bolt from a crossbow.

"Guards! Stop that cat!" yelled the king. But, it was too late. The clever cat was already gone.

"So what's the plan, you foul scarer of cats?" asked the queen. "Why do you want us to be invisible all of a sudden? You're not trying to take over Camelot again, are you?"

"My king and queen! How could you ever accuse me of such a thing?" Merlin was wounded and a terrific actor. Arthur and Guinevere simply frowned. After a long uncomfortable silence, the wizard continued. "My plan is a simple one: we're gonna become invisible and creep into the enemy camp. Once inside we'll sneak around and cause complete chaos!"

"Cause chaos?" said Arthur. "You have quite the talent for that! What do you have in mind this time?"

"Oh many, many things." Merlin thought for a moment and scratched at his long beard. "Putting things where they shouldn't be. Moving objects through the air. Leaving misty breath on their mirrors. General mischief like that! With a bit of luck, the enemy might think Camelot is haunted... then the fun really starts."

"Count me out!" said Guinevere, who did not think that sneaking around was a very queenly way to behave. "Someone should defend the castle and I volunteer me."

"Oh, go on my lady, please," begged Merlin. "We need as many haunted hands as we can get!"

One quick spooking and they'll run from the battlefield screaming like babies! Plus not a single drop of blood will be spilled, guaranteed!"

"Shame. Spilled blood could be useful right about now, especially if it isn't mine," protested Arthur (in the past, Lancelot would do most of the spilling and Arthur would turn up later to take the credit). "The enemy army has brought along some very scary creatures and I don't think I can persuade them to take up knitting."

"Well I'm sorry to disappoint you," growled the wizard. "But I cannot stand cruelty to magical creatures. As a wizard, I am sworn to protect them."

This announcement took Arthur and Guinevere by surprise. Merlin had sworn many things in his lifetime but had followed up on very few of them. 'Merlin Oathbreaker' had been his nickname at wizarding school. There was a famous incident where Merlin had betrayed over twenty people in one night and still didn't get a job in the pixie kingdom. Little did the king and queen know, many of the magical creatures were Merlin's best customers.

"Were-cows are an endangered species," the wizard added for emphasis.

"And I hear they are low in calories," thundered Guinevere. "According to your latest fast food restaurant?" She read from his takeaway menu. "Farmer Merlin's Grub Tub – try our were-cow supreme with brand new special sauce (the special sauce was more were-cow, but in liquid form).

"It's complicated," huffed Merlin. "I am cursed by a witch to be very greedy." (The wizard had used that one before).

"Maybe you are, Merlin," said Arthur shaking his royal head in frustration. "But this is the most bone-headed plan I have ever heard, and you're supposed to be wise. Why can't you destroy them with a spell?"

"I am sworn to–" began Merlin.

"Oh forget it!" yelled the king. Arthur groaned out loud. It looked like he would be going on a night raid against millions of scary soldiers with only his queen and cheating tennis doubles partner for company.

Chapter 24
The Not-So-Secret Secret Door

The moon had risen early – so early, in fact, that flocks of pigeons squabbled in their nests over what time it really was. They chirped and tweeted in anger above the grey walls of Camelot castle. No bird agreed with its neighbour. Feathers were ruffled. Eggs were thrown. Things turned ugly. Even Sir Softpaws tried to help and find common ground between the fighting flocks. Having eaten enough food already, he was not hungry for birds this time and instead tried his hardest to bring peace. But the pigeons would not listen. They had trusted cats before and their efforts had met with disastrous results. Softpaws claimed (in cat language) that being the biggest, mightiest creature Camelot had seen had given him a brand new point of view. Alas, the birds were too busy fighting over what o'clock it actually was to care.

Anyway, it was seven in the evening. Now back to the story...

Down below where humans liked to walk, a strange yellow mist seemed to ooze out of the cracks in the kingdom's cobblestone streets and drift up above head height. The gas was Merlin's doing. Being invisible hadn't stopped him from being a showman. The gas gave the mission an eerie atmosphere and helped build suspense. He would have preferred to make his trademark 'dragon's breath' fog spell. Since he didn't have a dragon to hand (Merlin had been blackballed by the guild of flying reptiles), the wizard had to make do with the lesser 'cat's breath' mist instead. Its smell was foul, like an unclean litter tray.

"Why does all your magic smell like fish!?" asked a voice. It sounded angry.

"Quiet Gwinny!" hissed someone who was probably Arthur. "You're supposed to be invisible!"

The invisible Arthur sneaked onwards with a sinking feeling in his heart. Kings did not do much sneaking and his metal studded shoes clattered on the Camelot cobbles.

The sound was loud enough to briefly alert the guards, but they enjoyed tap dancing and the gentle rhythm of Arthur's clattering shoes sent them off to sleep.

"Well… that solves that," said Arthur, careful not to trip over a snoozing guard.

"Maybe our luck is about to change," whispered Merlin. He had just jinxed them.

The great oak gates of Camelot blocked their path. Their planks were bound with iron strips and studded with a thousand flat topped nails. Everything about them said 'you shall not pass!'

Arthur heaved his shoulder against the gate, strained every muscle in his body, and quickly collapsed. The gate refused to budge (in case you needed to know).

"Magic it open!" puffed a tuckered out Arthur. "Do it Merlin... I command you!"

"Sire. Only the guards can open our main gate," replied Merlin. "I'm sure someone has the key somewhere."

The three looked around and saw hundreds of Camelot guards snoring heavily on the floor. Thanks to Arthur's shoes, not a man was left standing.

"Which one do you think has it?" said the queen.

The guards wore the exact same uniform, down to the helmet and badge. Since they all looked alike, finding the key-bearer would take all night. Plus, they were cuter than baby angels while they slept and nobody wanted to disturb them.

"Well, how about a spell where we could simply walk through the gate?" said Arthur. "Shouldn't be too hard for a seasoned wizard like yourself?"

"I can try, sire. But now is no time to go swimming." Merlin pointed through the gate. On the other side was at the ten metre drop into the castle moat. There was still no drawbridge. Arthur hadn't gotten around to ordering a new one (which, thanks to the invasion, turned out to be a really good idea). But for now it was quite inconvenient.

"Rats!" said Arthur, snapping his invisible fingers.

"And moat fish," added Merlin. "They can give you quite a nasty nip."

"Why don't we try the side door?" said Guinevere. "It's really handy when you want to leave Camelot without causing a fuss."

"Good idea!" chimed Merlin. "I almost forgot, we can use the secret side door."

Arthur stared at the queen in disbelief but remembered she was invisible. He was too, meaning Guinevere couldn't see the shocked look on his face.

"You mean there's a secret door? In the wall of my castle?" he snapped.

"It's not particularly secret," said the queen. "More of a need-to-know door, that's a little on the small side. You couldn't fit a horse through it, not without some grease and a lot of parsnips."

"Why wasn't I told about this?" snapped Arthur.

"We didn't think you'd like it," said a low soothing voice. It was either a high pitched Merlin or low-pitched Guinevere. The whole invisibility thing was getting really confusing.

"You're right about that!" hissed Arthur. "It makes a total mockery of our defences. What's the point of having a solid oak gate with a thousand iron studs if you can just nip around the side? What were you thinking?"

"Shopping mostly," said the wizard. "You know how tricky getting this and that can be when the castle is under siege…"

"And it's so annoying waiting for the guards to open the big gate, when you only need to pop out for a few bits and bobs..." agreed Guinevere.

"OK! OK! OK!" OK-ed the king with mild fury. "I think I can forgive and forget about this side door business. All may yet be well… as long as this is the last secret you're keeping from me."

"Of course." Both the queen and wizard were obviously fibbing.

So the three invisible heroes snuck around the side of a large castle turret and fumbled for the secret door in the dark. At last they found it. The small wooden door had been painted stone grey to blend in with the castle walls. However, the sign saying 'Don't Tell Arthur!' was coloured white and covered in red exclamation marks. The king frowned but kept his opinions to himself.

With a slow creek, Arthur pulled open the well-known secret door and they all crept through a small passageway to outside. Unfortunately, the walls were covered in grease and many mouldy parsnips had been left out.

"Urrrgh!" spluttered Guinevere, trying to hold her invisible nose and missing.

The last person to use the passageway had been Lancelot. He had wanted to go riding through the woods with his thirteen favourite horses. The last five had strongly objected to being squeezed through such a small passageway. It took extra parsnips to convince them otherwise.

Finally Arthur, Guinevere and Merlin arrived outside Camelot's great wall. Across the field, Merlin's cat's breath mist was growing thicker. It created a carpet of yellow gas and the wizard had been right – their secret entrance was so much cooler now. If it wasn't a secret mission, Merlin would have added some fireworks for maximum cool.

So, onwards they crept, each tip-toeing step took them past many foes and one toe closer towards the enemy camp.

Chapter 25
Because We're Ghosts, Guys

Camelot's surroundings were brimming with Oither & Co., Arteur & Co., Halfer & Co., and little Arty & Co. (who asked to be near the front where the best fighting would be). The four kings had come fully prepared for a fight and pitched their tents in a series of little villages.

Each little village flew their king's banner. Oither's camp had an image of a fat owl holding a fishing rod before a bubbling Cumbrian lake. For Arteur, it was two dolphins juggling hardened cheeses. Halfer proudly showed off his dwarf roots and flew a silver pickaxe on a black background of a dark cave. Last but not least, Arty's army fought under a flag of King Arty ordering the flag to be knitted of him ordering the flag to be knitted of him ordering the flag to be knitted. If you looked at his flag long enough, you would get dizzy and fall over.

For the most part, the enemy had spent the night partying and being overconfident. They were certain of victory and felt trying 100% was for dorks. After much fun, the knights had crept back to their comfy pavilions, whilst the ordinary men at arms were sleeping next to camp fires. Magical creatures were free to come and go as they pleased. There would be some sore heads and grey eyes at the big, meaty sausage-filled camp breakfast the following morning.

King Oither's Cumbrian builders had built a network of roads leading through the camp. Being organised and handy folk, they'd roped off wide paths between the tent villages. Their paths were so easy to follow that even a tipsy troll could find his way home on the second try. This meant that Arthur, Guinevere and Merlin were able to make fast progress into the heart of the enemy camp.

Apart from avoiding the gangs of archers singing rude songs with dark knights, and slipping by the occasional war-elephant, the journey had been a breeze. Although the invisibility spell was working perfectly, it still felt very weird to be tip toe-ing past the enemy, especially since nobody could actually see their toes.

"How did you ever talk me into this, Merlin?" muttered the king, almost tripping over a green dragon that was playing noughts and crosses with a dwarf.

"Easy-peasy, sire. You never give up, even when you should. Sometimes, we beg you."

Arthur hoped that was Merlin's voice behind him.

"Shush you two, they'll hear us," whispered an invisible Guinevere (aka Gwinvisible).

"No, we won't!" whispered a dwarf as the green dragon put a final circle in the middle box, bringing his winning streak to ten. The dwarf flipped the board over in a rage. He should have known better than to take on a dragon at board games.

"Oh no! We've been discovered!" moaned Arthur in a pained whisper.

"Don't panic," said Merlin, producing an old leather bag from underneath his robe. Just as the dwarf reached for his axe and the dragon inhaled, the wizard had found a memory erasing spell commonly known as a large rock. One swift whack and the dwarf and the dragon were sound asleep. When they woke up, they wouldn't remember a thing.

Eager for a pillage, Merlin rested his bag on a nearby stump and helped himself to anything the dragon and dwarf had in their pockets. From the bag, Merlin rummaged around his potions until he pulled out a telescope. The spyglass floated in the air as the invisible wizard scanned the enemy camp.

"That way, sire. We head west between the dog houses for werewolves and the troll den."

"Well done, Merlin." chortled Arthur. He looked at the noughts and crosses board. "Checkmate", he said, putting a cross in a square and somehow losing. Merlin and Guinevere simply tutted.

The three spies sneaked down the road feeling relieved. However, none of them noticed Merlin's bag still sitting on the tree stump where the wizard had forgotten all about it.

Before the bright moon had fully risen as bright moons tend to do, the three invisible sneakers had made their way to the heart of the camp. They searched row upon row of soldiers' tents for any sign pointing out where kings may be sleeping – a crown on a flag, guards outside, a double-decker tent, anything. After what seemed like hours of searching, the trio discovered a tent with four golden crowns stitched on the side. They slipped past the guards who were busy counting stars.

Inside this rather flashy looking tent, all four enemy kings were sound asleep and accounted for. From the empty plates and chunks of leftover bundt cake, they had helped themselves to a midnight feast and had gone to bed soon after. Together, these four vile fiends had agreed to divide Camelot among themselves. Then they were going to put lots of money into inventing a catapult big enough to sling Arthur into outer space. Their crude drawings on a nearby blackboard confirmed this. Arthur, Merlin and Guinevere stood silently, watching them.

The first king they spotted was Arteur from the French kingdom of Camembert. He was a chunky, ridiculous man who slept with three baguettes and a wedge of fresh onion to ward off evil spirits. His belly was covered in many different crumbs, ranging from pickle sandwiches to chocolate biscuits. If he ever fell out of bed, there would be nothing stopping him from rolling and rolling and rolling until he splashed down in the sea.

Next to him was Oither from the Lake District's Ca'elot kingdom. This king was tall, lean and not particularly bothered about personal hygiene. Out of his mouth stuck the tail end of a trout and fish bones were lodged in his thick scraggly bush of bright ginger hair. He looked like a rusted drain pipe with his feet sticking out from underneath the covers. Worse still, he had a reputation for plain speaking and even plainer thinking.

Then, there was Halfer from the dwarf kingdom. At least that was what his name above the bed said. For all Arthur and company knew, two dusty pillows that smelt of wet coal could have been snoring very loudly in bed. Whatever was under the sheets seemed to be picking its nose with a sharp pickaxe and mumbling about digging out rubies. He spoke in his sleep and said clearly in his native dwarf tongue, "Hi-ho, hi-ho, hi-ho, hi-ho."

Finally there was the young pup, King Arty. Although only a child, he had the violent temper of an old man who had lost his duck pond. A golden letter 'A' was written on both his pillows and his bed was covered in the finest plastics to keep the mattress safe from any accidents. At the moment, he was making gnashing noises and growling viciously. It was as if he was dreaming of ruling an ice cream kingdom and the chipmunks who lived there weren't allowed to have any. All the ice cream belonged to him.

"Right!" whispered Arthur. "On my count, let's make a lot of noise and pretend to be ghosts."

"Got it. Time for a big boo," whispered Guinevere quietly.

"Yes, your ghostly kingliness," whispered Merlin in an even quieter voice.

On the count of one, two, three, they booed and whooed and made a lot of noise.

At that, every king jolted out of bed and reached for their weapons.

"Wh-who goes there?" whimpered Arteur, quivering like a leaf.

"I-I'm so scared!" joined in Oither, wobbling like jelly.

"I want to go home!" added Arty, shaking like a snake.

"G-g-go away!" offered Halfer, shivering like a snowflake.

Arthur picked up a chain and began to rattle it around. He ran around the tent and flipped over anything he could find that wasn't nailed down.

"Woooo!" wooed Arthur. "I'm a ghost. I command you to leave Camelot and never return. Whooo, I'm a ghost. Whooo."

"No, you're not!" replied Halfer. "You're King Arthur and you appear to be naked!"

"Whoo? I mean, what?" squealed Arthur in a panic.

Arthur turned to see his reflection in the mirror. Sure enough, much of him had returned to being visible. Unfortunately, his clothes hadn't got the memo and remained invisible. To the uninformed bystander, he was indeed naked.

"Put some clothes on man!" growled an offended Oither. "What kind of king goes creeping around with nothing on?"

"It must be some kind of fashionable new kind of ambush," said Arty, shielding his eyes. "I think I read about it in Knights and Armour Magazine."

"Non, c'est le grande idiot Arthur!" said the French king.

"Get him!" they all agreed and charged at the nude Arthur with sharp weapons.

Arthur tried to flee, but it was no use. He cried out at the top of his voice, "Now Merlin! Now Guinevere! Save your king!" But there was no reply.

"Merlin? Merlin? Where are you?" he cried. But a reply there was not.

"Drat that confounded wizard!" he warbled. "Guinevere, help?"

His plea received no answer, except for the tent doors flapping open with the sound of running away. It could have been the wind, but it wasn't. Later, people swore they saw an empty dress and empty wizard's robe looking for hiding places.

Seeing no way out and being surrounded by three impressive swords and a small but menacing battle-axe, Arthur decided it was probably best for everyone if he surrendered and waited for his clothes to turn un-invisible.

Chapter 26
A Jail Cell Built For Two

Within moments of the invisibility potion wearing off, Arthur found himself captured and tied up like a pig at a hog roast. All that was missing was the pork gravy and the apple in his mouth. On the orders of four hopping mad monarchs, he was thrown into prison (built by Terry Cotter and associates) while they decided what was to be done about their nude intruder.

Feeling down in the dumpiest of dumps, Arthur counted pebbles once again and waited for his doom. On the brightish side, the king's clothes had slowly started to reappear. He could clearly see one glove and most of his long johns. When his socks returned, Arthur would only be half a tunic short of a complete outfit.

Many hours later, the prison door opened with a clang and somebody else stumbled into the cell, propelled by the boot of Lard the jailor. Lard had a knack for booting things. While this kick was not his personal best, his latest victim still flew a good ten metres before landing on its butt. This 'Somebody else' dusted himself off and rubbed his aching behind. He had also knocked over the king's pile of pebbles.

"Um… you haven't seen my bag anywhere, have you?" called the 'somebody'. "It's brown, weathered, and filled with a whole lot of dangerous potions?"

It was Merlin. The wizard had been captured a few hours later than Arthur had expected. After trying to slip a pixie five gold coins and hoping he'd look the other way, the crafty conjuror was double-crossed and sent straight to jail.
"I'll give you three gold coins for the safe return of that bag," Merlin offered.

Only a complete fool would be stupid enough to reunite the wizard with his potions – Lard the jailor was a complete fool but unfortunately the wizard's request fell on deaf ears. Lard had already slammed the cell door shut. He'd swallowed the key too, something he would later regret.

"Merlin!" yelped Arthur. But the penny dropped and the king returned to glum-town. "I was just about to say that it was good to see you, but–"

"It's good to see you too, my Lord," said the wizard. "Or it would be, if this jail cell wasn't so dark, I mean."

"I suppose if you're locked up in here with me, this isn't some clever escape plan?"

"Correct as ever, my lord," said Merlin, as useless as ever.

"And when will Guinevere be joining us?" asked Arthur.

The wizard drew his hands up into the long sleeves of his weather-strained robe and pulled out a crystal ball. He waved his hands as a thick mist filled the glass. When the mist had cleared, there was a snake-like creature with a hamster's face and giraffe's feet. It gave an evil laugh and disappeared. Merlin tutted and shook his head.

"According to the spirits, she'll be captured in about 30 minutes," said the wizard.

Chapter 27
Queen Seeks Smelly Horse

Thanks to all the excitement, the enemy camp was now on high alert. Soldiers dashed from tent to tent looking for any intruders. Knights mounted their horses and began searching the surrounding area. Witches took to their broomsticks and roamed the sky (while the ones who couldn't fly did some house work). Even big bulking trolls were splitting big bulking stones in half – just in case an intruder was hiding underneath. Soon, there was not an inch of camp left unsearched, unpoked, nor unprodded.

Just because their victory was certain, that was no excuse for sloppy security. The enemy army outnumbered the Camelotians in every way imaginable, but they had their pride. This intrusion had bruised it. Making sure everyone heard them, King Oither sent out clear orders about the intruders and what was to be done when they were found. The word was clear and simple. Any remaining trespassers were likely cold, afraid, lost, invisible and possibly crying. No mercy!

"Orders from the top, men. Keep an eye out for anyone invisible," said a sergeant with good comic timing. This drew a loud laugh from the rest of the men. "I'm serious. King Oither said so!"

"There's another one for your joke book, sergeant!" suggested a man whose sides had split.

It was gossiped about among the soldiers that the sergeant was working on a book – *The Extremely Stupid Sayings of King Oither the Obvious*. The sergeant would not say (not until his publisher had paid him an advance). For an added joke, the men sent over 128 reports claiming they had seen 'invisible intruders who were up to no good'.

It was nearing morning as a cold mist rose from a lonely stream far away from any soldiers. Something funny was happening on the bank involving an invisible woman and how lost she really was. With how similar everything looked in the night time, and how quickly she had rushed for her own safety, Guinevere finally realized she was still trapped behind enemy lines (and the great distance those lines went back). There was a chilly wind blowing and the queen couldn't wait for her next warm fireplace. Marshmallows would be a good add-on too. She wasn't sure how long the invisibility spell would last, but her love of heat and sweets would be forever.

Guinevere hopped over many hedges and fences, looking for anything that would aid her quest to figure out where the heck she was (sometimes she had accidentally jumped the same fence twice). So, chewing on a piece of straw to help her concentrate, the queen planned her next move and how to achieve it. With Camelot looking like it had had its chips and Arthur under lock and key, her options were few.

By a stroke of luck, the queen came across the stables housing Whiffy the horse. His home was far away from Camelot's other horses after they kept complaining about his smell. Thankfully, the enemy guarding him had the same complaint and weren't to be seen for miles. Guinevere crept up on the stables making sure she didn't make a sound. Opening the doors very slowly and stepping on a few pieces of leftover gingerbread from chapter 7, the queen had just found her next ally.

Watching the horse chow down on some fantastic hay, Guinevere softly patted him on his mane. Whiffy let out a terrified "neigh!" and slammed two horseshoes through the stable wall.

"It's only me, you stinky horse!" whispered the queen.

Whiffy didn't know who 'me' was, but considering 'me' couldn't be seen, he decided to do what he was told. The invisible woman climbed aboard his back (Whiffy hoped it wasn't a ghost of a rider haunting him for his horsey misdeeds). With a damsel-like "Yaaarrrrrgh!" Guinevere kicked the stirrups and her steed bolted from his stables. Together they rode off, still without a plan.

Chapter 28
Queen Seeks Scribe

After many hours riding along the main road, Guinevere finally reached a 'refreshments' area. Merlin had built it miles from Camelot in case Arthur found out. There were a lot of shops and places to get a quick bite to eat. Each had a cute, cuddly mascot to help part a tourist from his or her cash. Unfortunately, the morning was so early that not a single shop was open.

Guinevere spotted a branch of a nasty fast-food chain called *Farmer Merlin's Grub Tub*. There was a large poster advertising Merlin's 'new and improved' Were-cow burgers. However, the restaurant had been closed for some time. The Were-cows had joined the enemy army and were seeking better working conditions. So it looked as if there would be no royal breakfast for the queen.

After walking by a large shop window filled with Sir Softpaws dolls (each had his trademark catchphrase 'meow'), and some half-price King Arthur costumes for Halloween, the queen decided to stop for a rest and a quick wash and brush up. With all that running about and crossing rivers, she was starting to smell like a barn. For once, the horse could not be blamed.

Guinevere had just finished washing her face in a public fountain when she caught sight of some clothing shops. Their styles were too flashy for her refined oyal taste, but the invisibility spell was beginning to wear off fast. She didn't want anyone to see that her dress had been ruined by layers of mud and other stuff. So, with a queenly boot to the door, she broke into the closest clothes shop that wouldn't make her look like a rainbow pineapple.

"Oh no! Not like this," she thought. The queen searched again, and again, and again. "Nobody suffers in Camelot half as much as I do," she hummed as she ruffled through piles of clothes. Leaving rather too few coins for the tailor, out came Guinevere in her new yellow cloak, white leather belt, and shiny green ankle boots. She winced, longing for her familiar silk gowns instead of this ridiculous yellow outfit. Instead of a pineapple, she looked more like a walking buttercup.

At the far end of the refreshment area, she spotted a hut without a chimney. There were wisps of grey smoke coming from an unplanned hole in the roof. It was painted the welcoming colour of black. A sign above the door read: "Inky The Scribe" Words and Stuff. This gave Guinevere an idea (probably her best idea of the book so far).

"Yoo hoo!" yoo hooed the queen in a loud voice. With her dainty hands, she hammered the door so hard that the paint chipped. When there was no answer, Guinevere decided to enter anyway and stepped into the hut. She would make her apologies later and offer to pay for the door.

The place was halfway to a hovel and twice as dank as a dungheap. Piles of yellowing paper covered every wall. The floor was covered in messy splodges of ink, paint, and chalk. Just then, a skeleton-like figure with a shiny bald head emerged from the shadows and spoke in a low whisper.

"Got anything that needs writing?" he asked. "A sign for your dairy farm? An advert for your eagles? Some naughty words that only wizards know? I writes it all, I does."

Guinevere turned up her nose at his terrible grammar. "If he writes as bad as he speaks," she thought, "I's ams really in right proper trouble."

This scribe had already offended her. With her new yellow outfit on, surely he could tell that she didn't work in a dairy farm? The crown on her head should have told him that she was a high-born and noble customer, not a milkmaid.

The queen cleared her throat.

"Good day to you scribe. I require your services."

"Happy to help you, I am," said Inky, annoying the queen with his word order again. He offered her chair and she sat down, but not before she'd removed a stack of comics about a mouse and a goat who solve crime together.

The scribe picked his nose with the feather end of his quill and dipped it in the pot. It was empty. Muttering under his breath he poked around in a cluttered drawer, trying to find a new bottle of ink and more paper.

"Take this down immediately," ordered Guinevere. "Queen available. Experienced ruler of major kingdom. Excellent track-record of managing peasants, plagues, and wizards..."

"A thousand pardons, your highness, miss," interrupted the

scribe. He scratched his scalp with a long fingernail. "But what is this all about, for sure?"

"Hmm," thought Guinevere, keeping her secrets to herself. "Think of it as... a list."

"A list you say?" said the scribe.

The queen nodded. "Yes, a special kind of list. I would like four copies in your best handwriting, please. One in French. One in high Cumbrian. One in local Dwarf. Oh, and one with a couple of cute pictures of swords and crowns for young children."

Inky looked hard at Guinevere trying his best to figure out what she was up to. With the current trouble going on in the kingdom, why would someone come to his shop for such a strange task? So early in the morning too. Normally, people just wanted fan mail addressed to Sir Softpaws. Some wanted poems, dedicated to Sir Softpaws. A few odd folk wanted letters promising troughs of milk and houses full of salmon if 'he' ever visited (the 'he' in question being Sir Softpaws). Finally, the scribe began to understand.

"Ah! I see," said Inky, wise to her plan and wagging his finger to prove it. "You plan to give those four list to the four foreign kings and..."

"Please, good scribe!" interrupted the queen. "Aren't you going to help a woman in need?"

He would receive a rap from her damsel's fist if he said 'no'.

"I'll help," said Inky. "But first I must ask you a few questions."

"Very well. Carry on," replied Guinevere. "But keep the tone serious and formal, please. Oh! And put a splash of perfume on them. That way they'll know I've got standards."

So Inky asked Guinevere many questions and quickly found out about her impressive life experience.

"How many jobs have you had?" he asked.

"One," declared the queen.

"What's your the best quality?"

"Royalness."

"If there be one thing you would change about yourself, what would that one thing be..."

Chapter 29
Queen Seeks Revenge

"Presenting Arthur, former king of Camelot," announced a snooty minstrel dressed in brilliant purple tights. He parped his horn with a poofy blart and parped one more time when nothing happened. Missing his cue to march, Arthur was led through the enemy camp past many bad folk who did not wish him well. The king took his place on a platform before the four mean kings. Much like a bunch of villains, they sat before him on their thrones and had the same expression as a zoo lion finding his cage unlocked.

In the grey and boring light of morning, Kings Oither, Arteur, Halfer, and Arty had gathered to decide what should happen to last night's surprise visitor (whose clothes thankfully were no longer invisible). Many henchmen had come along too, eager for a front row seat when Arthur learned his fate.

"I wonder if I'll get a fair trial," mumbled Arthur like a fool. Then a gruff man with a heavy axe forced him to his knees as the four kings sneered at him from some very fluffy cushions.

Sensing just a little bit of danger, Arthur began to do what he did best – bluff. "Ah ha! Good to see you again," he smirked at the kings. "I wondered when you'd want to seek peace."

At that, millions and millions of voices laughed at the big hopes of one little man.

"Very well," he continued. "What do you say? How about I give you double goody-bags for my next birthday? You can't say fairer than that. I'll throw in a free game of pin the tail on the wolf."

"Flattery won't save you this time," chuckled Oither, before he added. "Former King Arthur!"

"Former king? Already? That was quick!" muttered Arthur. He did not like the sound of the word 'former' and had deliberately ignored the snooty minstrel in purple tights from earlier.

"It fits," came a voice out of nowhere. At first, Arthur thought it was a ghost playing tricks, but then realized the voice was king Halfer's, struggling to be seen beneath a large throw cushion.

"Not to me, it doesn't," said Arthur. "Why not former...ly captured and currently...ly back home having a good time king Arthur. Rolls off the tongue nicely, doesn't it?"

"Shall we get on with the trial?" grumbled Oither in a grim voice. He rose from his chair like a crumpled crow and addressed Arthur directly. Reading from a parchment from his little book of rules, Oither began. "Former King Arthur, you stand here accused of being rude, mean-spirited, treating clowns unfairly, and throwing a very bad birthday party. These are most serious crimes. Former King Arthur, how do you plead?"

"Angry!" roared Arthur, angrily.

"Nope. You're not allowed to plead 'angry'!" said Arty. "It's got to be innocent or guilty."

"Even I know that," added Arteur. Back in Brittany, the execution would have been over by now. Then there would have been feasting, romance, and heroic tales of heroes without tails. "France was the best," he thought as he longed for home.

Then Halfer chimed in. "Hmm. I suppose angry rhymes with guilty."

This they all agreed. Rhyming was as good as a confession.

"Very good," said Oither. And he wrote 'guilty' in the parchment.

"Oh poop," pleaded Arthur.

The enemy army agreed this was a good thing. There was a rush of people trying to get onto the platform. Everyone wanted to volunteer to be Arthur's executioner. They waved his insulting letters – sent when he thought he could rely on the services of a certain Green Knight. Others waved pictures of a clown with "Justice for Funnynuggets" written below. Whatever their outrage, there was an ocean of papers united against Camelot's king. In recent days, Arthur had been running low on friends. What few allies the king had left, he would have to send a gift basket of thanks (with a chocolate Excalibur – the fruit and nut ones weren't so bad).

"Wait!" cried a voice. "Let me pass, I have written-down words to speak!"

Arthur was surprised to see an odd stranger push his way through the crowd at the platform's edge. The man certainly didn't look like an angel. In fact, dressed entirely in black, he looked more like Death himself. His long fingernails curled around four neatly-wrapped parchment scrolls. A faint glimmer of hope rose in Arthur's heart. Had the mysterious man come to save him?

"What is the meaning of this, you gangly ghoul?" cried king Arty in a rage.

"Let me pass! For I have words to speak," repeated the lanky stranger, waving his scrolls with a flourish.

Arthur's heart did a somersault and nearly jumped out his mouth. What could be written on those scrolls? Recipes for custard creams? A drawing of a badger? Not royal pardons – surely? Had Arthur written them himself earlier to save his own skin? Maybe. He had forgotten all about his insulting letters from earlier. Was the king actually allowed to pardon himself? He hoped the answer was 'yes'.

"Who are you and what do you want?" barked Arteur. "Be quick. We have important business to get on with, non?"

"My lords, I am Inkitiktaktellious," said the stranger. "Simple folk call me Inky. And my business is delivering these precious letters..."

With another flourish he presented three of the kings with a personalised scroll. They smelt wonderful. Very flowery.

"Is there one for me?" called a voice from out of nowhere. It was Halfer again. He had fallen off his chair. Spotting a tiny hand reaching out, Inky handed him the final scroll in local dwarfish.

Oither had already broken the seal on his scroll and was scanning its words. Soon every king was reading their scroll with casual interest. After a brief silence, Oither turned to Inky.

"You can tell Queen Guinevere her services will not be needed," he declared.

"Yeah, girls are icky," said Arty. "No girls allowed in my palace."

Arthur's face fell like an elephant off a cliff.

"What?!" he cried in shock and despair. It seemed that Guinevere was looking for greener pastures and a brand new king and husband.

"But sires!" protested Inky. "This queen is an experienced ruler. She's a wise monarch. And she commanded me to be reminding you that she comes with her own crown jewels. You can't say fairer than that!"

"Pass," said Arteur. "She is a little desperate, non?"

"I'm out too," said Halfur. "We dwarves know when a women is trying to pull the wool over our eyes."

"Hey!" yelled Arthur, reminding everyone he was still here and still annoyed.

A little flustered, Inky unravelled another scroll and read its contents.

"And if the kings refuse my offer..." continued the scribe. "The queen commands me remind them that she is praised for her tremendous beauty. Also, she knows where all the gold of Camelot be hidden."

Arthur buried his head in his royal hands. Had it really come to this? As her next act of betrayal, Guinevere would probably tell them all about his shameful love of brussel sprouts.

With hands the size of silver dinner plates, Oither crunched his scroll into a small ball.

"Not today thank you!" he said.

"But – protested Inky, afraid that the queen would go through with her promise to melt him down into ink if he returned with 'no' for an answer.

"But nothing!" snapped the blunt talking Cumbrian King. Then he hurled his crumpled scroll at the scribe. The other kings followed suit, screwing up their scrolls and throwing them at Inky. Arty's scroll zipped over the scribe's shoulder and landed in a pile of dung next to a farmer's cart. Shortly afterwards it was eaten by a passing goat.

The crowd booed as the skeletal scribe was led outside to be thrown into the moat. All eyes (and pelted fruit) were on him, so nobody noticed the figure in the bright yellow cloak hidden behind the barrels of lemons and cheese. She glared at the four kings with anger hotter than a million mustard curries. None of them had even bothered to take her C.V. seriously.

"I'll have my revenge!" she muttered under her breath. "You'll regret the day you insulted Guinevere, queen of… Camelot, for now." At that, she twirled her yellow cape and stropped away outside.

Chapter 30
King Arthur Is Boring!

After a short 'moat-throwing' break, the four kings returned to debating what should be done about Arthur. His sentence may have been 'guilty', but there was no fair way to decide who should execute him. Arthur's clothes-free one-man attack was a surprise they were trying to forget. Still, it had made Arthur almost too easy to capture. Each king had prepared himself for a long fought battle. Nobody thought the punishment stage of the fun would come this quickly. So the four spent a long time sitting on their thrones and swapping deadly ideas that would make them all happy (except Arthur, who had a splinter from the wooden platform).

"Feed him to a dragon?" suggested Arteur. "They cost a lot to feed, non?"

"Why should a big reptile have all the fun?" butted in Arty. "I think we should have a game of bingo. Full house gets the first blow."

"Everyone knows you rig the balls," shot back Halfer. "We could put everyone in a queue, give them a sword and blindfold, and take turns whacking. Could be fun."

"Where are we going to get a million blindfolds from?" snapped Oither.

"How about we let him go?" came a gruff voice. Arthur was speaking into his sleeve and hoping he could sway their decision. The kings glared at him and Arthur was silent once more.

Arteur sighed. "If I knew Le Arthur was this easy to catch you, why did I even bring my army? We came by boat, you know. The seasickness? Tres terrible!"

"I agree," added Halfer. "This is just embarrassing. Dwarves shouldn't be above ground for this long. Why don't we just turn Arthur into blackcurrant jam?"

"Not a bad idea. I know some witches who bake," said Oither.

"How about we starve him a little?" asked Arty. "We can get started on a punishment right away and see how we feel about it later."

The kings agreed to disagree. Then they went away to have a spot of lunch. When the kings came back, they pretty much said the same things as before. But, with a double-helping of roast beef, they had enough pep in their step to say the same things even louder. Somebody forgot to feed Arthur, so Arty had gotten his way for now.

As for the armies of the four kings, they had gotten really bored. To pass the time, they organised a high stakes game of leapfrog. Together they formed a snaking line around the camp that went into the millions of bent-over players. Most of the hoppers had badly hurt their knees before they were halfway done. Many earned themselves a one-way ticket to the hospital.

The four kings were locked in debate when in came Merlin, dressed as a royal cupbearer. He carried many goblets on a silver tray and a small wooden barrel on his back. The old wizard served the kings some light refreshments. Arthur's face went red as angry blood rushed through his royal veins.

"Merlin?" Arthur snapped, "Why are you betraying me?"

"Sorry, Sire. But I've gotta go where the winners are," said the wizard. He turned to his new masters. "Would you like to see the wine menu? We have a particularly fruity vintage..."

"Treachery!" shrieked Arthur at the top of his voice.

"Treachery? Yes. New job opportunity? Also, yes." Merlin replied without a hint of shame.

"More wine, cupbearer!" cried Oither. "And, while you're at it, give my boots another licking. You missed a bit of dirt last time."

Merlin knelt down and gave each foot a gentle scrub with a well worn rag. Then he buffed each boot with his beard until they shone. When he was finished, the wizard merrily planted a kiss on Oither's tootsies. "A thousand thank you's, your most kingly kingness," he creeped. "Have I told you how much I love working for you?"

"Leave!" grunted Oither.

"Great joke, your highness. Best I ever heard." Merlin laughed and skipped away.

"I'd like my death sentence now, please," moaned Arthur. He swallowed a little bit of sick.

"Awww! He's spoiling the surprise!" snapped young King

Arty.

"Looks like Arthur has no more friends left," laughed Halfer.

"Yes, he is 'King Arthur No Friends'." Arteur joined in.

"Isn't that punishment enough?" Arthur tried to sob but he could never cry on cue.

"No!" the four chorused.

"Well, rats to what you think," said Arthur. "At least, my cat hasn't turned his back on me."

Arthur said these words with confidence, but quickly looked around to see if Sir Softpaws hadn't joined them as a squire or cook's assistant or something with room for promotion. With a sigh of relief, at least Arthur's cat seemed to have stayed loyal.

"Your cat? That is your only friend?" Arty teared up with mean chortles. "What a saddo!"

The four kings pointed and laughed at Arthur before they all yawned and ran out of puff. Thinking up ways to mash the bad birthday king sounded like a tonne of fun this morning. Now the task had dragged and dragged on for ages, it had become just like maths homework.

"Oh! Let's just throw him in jail and lose the key!" Arty was upset to learn he missed out on the world's longest leapfrog line.

"A good night's sleep would help me come up with gory ideas," said Halfer, using his beard as a pillow.

"It's true," added Arteur. "The naked idiot. He interrupted my eight hours of sleep. It's bad for the brain, non?"

"Very well," mumbled Oither. "We will meet again here tomorrow. Let us go to the camp kitchen for some warm milk and cookies."

At that, the kings departed, leaving Arthur all alone. Arthur waited until they were gone and tried to bite through his chains to freedom. Unfortunately, the gruff man with a heavy axe was still there. It so happens, he rather enjoyed being a guard. Arthur blew him a raspberry and made huffing sounds as an axe-handle prodded him towards jail.

Chapter 31
Grate Expectations

Arthur dangled in mid-air and not for the first time in this book. Once again, he was back in a dark, cold prison cell. Even the rats were shivering. Somewhere down the corridor, the guards were playing cards and roasting sausages of many sizes on a warm fire. There was no light except for the faint flickering of glowing pork from beneath the oak door.

Being short of a friend or two had bought the king some much-needed wriggle room, but the iron chains that bound him to the wall kept him from wriggling free. The king found this was becoming a familiar nuisance. He was starting to get a bit fed up. At least, Sir Softpaws was back at home sleeping in his basket. That was, unless he found Arthur's bed unguarded. The king had to face facts – his cat was fast asleep on the royal pillows, leaving fur everywhere.

Suddenly the cell exploded with light. The iron door swung open and a cloaked figure was lobbed in like a bundle of dirty laundry. Pulling himself upright on his chains, Arthur heard a familiar voice that was no stranger to jail time.

"Good evening, my lord and best friend!" Merlin said. "Lovely weather isn't it? Well, it might be if I was allowed outside."

"Back again already, Merlin?" Arthur groaned. "What happened to working for King Oither as a royal cupbearer and boot polisher?"

"I've been sacked," said Merlin, sadly.

"Oh dear!" said Arthur sarcastically. "Let me guess. You tried to steal Oither's cup when he wasn't looking."

"I didn't think he'd miss one," wailed the wizard. "I also gave that brat Arty too much lemonade before bedtime. You do not want to hear how that turned out." Merlin gave a nervous giggle. Arthur's tummy replied by making a loud grumble. From its point of view, it had been denied roast beef.

"You've got a lot of nerve being thrown in here," groaned Arthur. "You switched sides and joined my enemies. If I were you, I would fear the power of the royal wrath!"

"You're chained to a wall," said Merlin, reminding him. "That's the least of my worries."

"I don't suppose you've got any biscuits?" asked the hungry king. "If you could magic up a plate of custard creams they may help soothe the royal wrath." The wizard simply shook his head.

As Merlin's old eyes grew accustomed to the greyish-blackness of the jail, he began eyeing up possible exits.

"I expect you're thinking of trying to escape through that blocked up grate, aren't you?" said Arthur wearily. With a chained hand, he pointed a finger toward the barred window above them.

"Any reason why I shouldn't?" asked Merlin, searching the lining of his robe for any secret tools or spells. Since he had lost his special wizard bag full of potions, Merlin had been using anything he could find (whether it was magic or not was no longer important). "Those rusty iron bars are never going to budge without some teamwork, elbow grease, and a metal file or something." He got on his hands and knees and began searching the cell floor for anything sharp.

Just then, the duo heard a voice. "Cooie!" it said, in the sort of loud whisper you'd usually only hear in a bad school play. Arthur assumed the loud whispering was Merlin trying to talk to rats and strike a bargain for their help. "Another one of the things they taught you in wizard school," he thought.

"Cooie! It's me…" called a familiar voice. It was coming from outside the prison bars.

"No you're not, I'm me." The king was right. He was him.

"No, you... ugh, why do I even bother?" The familiar voice became familiarly annoyed. Edging closer to the bars, the figure pulled back her hood and revealed herself.

"Guinevere! All is forgiven!" cried Arthur in delight. "I can't believe you came back to rescue me. Have you got any biscuits?"

"Biscuits?" answered the Queen. "Absolutely not. Sitting on the throne all day is making you plump. When we're home, I'm putting you on the prison diet."

"Pass," Arthur said. "But you are here to rescue me, aren't you?"

"Not quite," said Guinevere.

"That means, you must have married some other king," said Arthur. "That's just cold, Gwinny."

"Wrong," said Guinevere. "They all said no. So I'm back on team Camelot to rain vengeance down on the lot of them."

"Just once," said Arthur. "Just once, I'd like to go on an adventure without everyone betraying me."

Without wasting any more time explaining things, Guinevere pushed a rather mouldy item through the bars (Arthur was a little miffed because he rather enjoyed explanations – they made the story easier to follow). The thing landed with a thump and covered the cell floor in glass bottles and paper packets of all shapes, sizes and colours. Guinevere had found Merlin's magic bag.

"Put them to good use, boys," crowed Guinevere. "Magic up something particularly horrid for those nasty old goats and little shrimp."

"Hey!!!" bellowed a gruff voice that did not belong to the queen. Soon came the frantic ringing of alarm bells, the shuffle of surprised feet, and some bad-natured shouting.

"Drat!" said Guinevere. "I've been spotted! Must fly!" In a moment, the queen was gone.

On the jail floor, one of the glass bottles was giving off a white luminous glow. Soon it began to float. A family of rats watched in amazement as the bottle slowly glided in Arthur's direction. It somehow sensed he needed feeding. The hungry king craned his neck out to grab the wonder by his teeth. But Merlin's arm darted from his sleeve faster than a striking snake and snatched the potion away from Arthur before he could drink it.

The bottle fell to the ground and shattered, its liquid formed a glowing green puddle on the stone slabs. One rat walked up, sniffed at the sticky mess, and was turned into stone. Jail cats would later chip their teeth on him.

"It's probably best if you don't drink anything without my say so," warned Merlin.

Arthur had turned a ghostly shade of pale.

"What in the name of Excalibur was in that potion!" cried the king. "I could have been rocked!"

"I'm not completely sure," muttered Merlin, collecting all the bottles and potions and arranging them in order of size.

"Don't you have a system for keeping track of your magical

potions and ingredients?" asked Arthur in amazement. "I mean, why not label them or something?"

"Never got around to it," Merlin muttered to himself. "Let's see. Was it again? Red. Red begins with an 'r', so red must stand for... strength."

"Pardon?" replied Arthur in disbelief.

Merlin uncorked the bottle and sniffed its contents. "Nope, that one's just ketchup."

"Unbelievable!" cried the king. "And people say wizards are supposed to be wise."

"Meh," shrugged Merlin. "I doubt they've ever met a real wizard."

"Well, I've met every wizard in Britain trying to shrink my cat," began Arthur. "And let me tell you Merlin, even though they were all useless, you are by far the smelliest, worst dressed, stupidest..."

Uncorking another bottle, Merlin dabbed two drops of blue goo onto a breadcrumb. He threw it towards a nearby rat who was minding his own business.

"Go on my little friend! Nummy nummy num num. Get that breadcrumb into your ratty tum tum," said the wizard, urging the rodent on. He turned to Arthur with a smug grin. "Watch this, sire, I think you'll be impressed."

The rat paused, sniffed the bread, and twitched a little.

"The Lancelot spell," said Merlin in delight. "One of my best. A single swig and you'll be undefeatable in battle. Plus, it combs your hair while you sleep."

The rat darted forward and gobbled up the breadcrumb.

"Avez-vous du fromage, mon cher?" it asked in a fluent french accent. Then a look of surprise came on its face as it began to float slowly towards the ceiling.

Arthur could not wag his finger at the wizard, as he was hanging from a hook in the wall. But he made his displeasure known by shaking his head in disappointment.

"So, good news!" said the wizard. "At least, we know it's not the blue potion."

Arthur stared into the wizard's bag. There were many, many colours and they were running out of rats.

"Got any more breadcrumbs… or rats?" he asked and batted his eyelashes hopefully.

Chapter 32
The Return of the Queen

Ducking and dodging flying spears, arrows, pitchforks and many other nasty stuff from the pursuing enemy, Guinevere and Whiffy the horse fled the enemy camp. The queen retreated with all the speed four frenzied hooves could ferry her. She had also forgotten she was no longer invisible. Soon, the pair had taken off down the path heading to Camelot and safety (for now, at least). What is more, Whiffy's natural gas provided the perfect smokescreen to escape the enemy and many were lost in his stenchy fog. Once free, the queen spurred the horse ever onward. In fact, he didn't need much spurring. He already had the wonderful smell of home in his nostrils. Home did not miss the terrible smell of him.

As Guinevere approached the gates of Camelot, she heard a sleepy voice call out from the castle walls. "Who goes there?" It was Old Bede above the gates. Arthur had demoted him to night watchman after one too many misunderstandings outside the Round Table room. The hard of hearing codger was no better than he had been many chapters earlier.

"I said, who goes there?" he said.

"Who do you think?" said the exasperated queen.

"That's why I'm asking," replied Old Bede. "If they tell me, I don't have to bother checking who goes there. Now, who goes there?" He idly picked his nose waiting for an answer.

"I'm the Queen," came the reply.

"Ian? Can't say I know any Ian. What's your business here, Ian?"

"No, you twit. I said I'm the Queen."

"You'd best not be planning any invasions, now Ian," threatened Bede. "My bones may be a little dusty but I can defend these walls as good as anyone half my age." At that, he threw a spear which landed in the moat with a wet 'plop'.

"It's Queen Guinevere. Guinevere! Guinevere! Don't you recognize the crown?" She had humoured Bede long enough.

"Queen Guinevere!" called the startled guard. He leapt to his feet in amazement. "What an honour. This is the first time

I've ever met a king or queen."

"No need to make a fuss," she said. But it was too late. Bede had already grabbed hold of his brass horn and started to blow frantically.

"I'll never forget this honour, your highness," he bellowed.

Unfortunately, the racket he was making soon got people's attention. In no time at all, an excited crowd rushed towards the castle gates and carried the queen and horse over the moat by hand.

"Our queen! Our queen has come to save us!" they cried as they spilled into the streets. Now Guinevere's way was blocked by wide-eyed Camelotians.

The glum folks of Camelot were desperate for any good news and the sight of their queen counted as such. For weeks and weeks, they had wondered about their fate. Without Arthur, Guinevere, Merlin, the knights, Sir Softpaws and anyone left in the kingdom who could read, they were without any leadership.

"Finally, some government at last," cried one. "About my carrots..."

"Nobody's collecting the bins," yelled another. "Is this poisonous?"

"Can somebody feed my dog?" another voice.

"Where's my pension?"

"I have a note."

"Do I have to learn a new language?"

My children haven't been to school."

"Isn't it a little bit cold?"

Soon Guinevere was swamped with requests and petitions from the working men and women from her kingdom, and was nearly overcome by an ocean of hands and noise.

"Um… About that whole 'coming to save you' thing…" began Guinevere, but she stopped herself, realising honesty would only make things worse. Her husband was the best liar in the family. Being married to him for so long, the queen could only dabble in lies. She had yet to reach his mastery of fibbing.

By a stroke of luck, a fat man with a rosy red face pushed forward and grabbed Whiffy by the reins.

"Make way for the queen or you'll all be spending

Christmas underground in irons and chains," he warned.

He was Ralph the Jailor (no relation to Lard) and he was joined by Guinevere's ladies in waiting. They began to poke random peasants and, with a stern booting from the noble ladies, a path was cleared for the queen.

"Where to, your highness?" Ralph asked, pushing an old man over a small garden wall.

"To the Dragon Burger cart, pronto," said the queen. "I'm starving. Then onto Excali-bar's for an extra large fruit juice. Then… I'll think of a plan."

Ralph nodded. The queen noticed his nose was very sunburnt. Spending his days in a dark dungeon, he wasn't used to sunlight. The fact he had left his familiar basement was a sign of desperate times.

"Wouldn't our Queen like to visit the Hospital first?" suggested lady-in-waiting number one. "Her knights have been bedridden for so long. They will have great need of you."

"Right now, I have great need of a Big Dragon sandwich," said the Queen, ignoring him. "I'm so hungry I could eat a horse."

"And you probably will if you buy a burger from that place," snorted lady-in-waiting number two.

Chapter 33
The Potion Commotion

Twenty minutes later, with her stomach filled with cheap meat and her dress lightly spattered with hot sauce stains, Gunievere made her way up the winding stone steps towards the hospital. When she entered the halls of healing, she was met with the sounds of many men groaning and other sickly sounds. The knights' injuries had been so bad yet they had still not recovered a jot. As she drifted by bed after bed, Guinevere was greeted by a strange voice.

"Saints be praised!" said someone muffled by bandages.

It was Sir Bors. He was wrapped up like a mummy from head to toe. Suddenly he sneezed, and realizing his bandages were caked in trapped snot, squealed out loud.

"Sir Bors!" Guinevere snapped, trying to work out whether he was infectious."You don't have the plague do you?"

"No, my lady."

"A dragon didn't burn you up like a roast sausage?"

"No, it didn't, my lady."

"You weren't slain by a troll horde or roaming gang of dark knights?"

"But my lady, you yourself were in the halls of healing only..."

"Then why aren't you out on the battlefield defending my city?" cried the queen. "And that goes for the rest of you too! Get up, get out there, and get clobbering my enemies!"

There was a groan from every bed as the knights helplessly shook their limbs.

"Our Queen! Our Queen has come with magical help for her heroic heroes!" cried an excited voice. It was the Head Healer.

"Head healer!" snapped Guinevere. "Why aren't these men aiding Camelot?"

The Head Healer thrust a pile of papers into her face. "Sick notes," he said. "Your knights are all wounded beyond belief. These notes say no medicine in the world can help them."

"Nonsense!" cried Guinevere. "You couldn't be more wrong if you tried."

At that, she slapped a leather bag on the table with a smug humph. Inside, many bright colours from many dusty bottles gave off an eerie glow.

"I know that sign anywhere!" Bors cried, looking at a red mark on the side of the bag. "It is Merlin's rune and no mistake!" It was not the wizard's mark. Rather, it was a spot of flaming hot sauce from Guinevere's Big Dragon sandwich. However, Bors was heading in the right direction, so she did not correct him.

"Right you are sir knight. Her Glorious Royalness has brought Merlin's magical medicine bag!" cried the Head Healer trying to snatch it from her hand. "With these magical medicines Camelot's finest knights will be fighting fit in no time!" Behind him, Sir Percival had an allergic reaction to buttered toast.

"Careful," warned the queen. "Merlin never bothers to label his spells. You don't know what you'll be getting."

"No matter," replied the knight. "I never bother to label the sharp end of my sword." He pointed at a bowl of oranges and a card reading 'Get Well Soon' which he assumed was his weapon. Clearly, Sir Bors hadn't gotten well enough.

The crowd of bandaged knights were closing in on the Head Healer and trying to snatch bottles from the bag. They were joined by eager knights from other wards. Soon, a free-for-all broke out with big men pushing and shoving each other in the name of magical medicine.

A misty green bottle was quickly snatched up by Sir Bedevere, but Sir Bors stamped on his hand and grabbed it before he was smashed on the head by Sir Gawain's walking stick. Sir Galahad attempted a diving slide to reach the medicine but Sir Cador had him in a headlock who was poked in the eye by Sir Kay who himself had Sir Gareth's teeth in his shin bone. Even though Sirs Cheatsalot, Shoutsalot, Pokesalot, and Losealot had formed a human wall, Sir Headstrong knocked them down like a bowling ball. Meanwhile, Sir Lid-shut charged into a nearby pillar by mistake. In the background, Guinevere calmly read a small book and waited patiently (this was not her first time watching the knights have a disagreement). Just then, Sir Tristan got a firm grip on the bottle, wrenching it from the white knuckled fist of Sir Hector. Letting out a shout of triumph, Sir Tristan thrust the bottle to his lips which were punched by Sir Geraint.

"Stop your madness! This is a house of healing" cried the Head Healer at the top of his voice.

Nobody took any notice. At last, Sir Bors made one final leap at the medicine but the bottle shattered in his hand Luckily he was wearing chain mail gloves or things could have turned ugly.

There was a short silence. Then the other knights let out a groan of disappointment.

"As usual, Sir Breaks Everything strikes again," said Sir Pokesalot.

"We were only playing," added Sir Bedevere.

"You're always too rough," snorted Sir Hector.

"Thanks for nothing, you oaf," said Sir Galahad for good measure.

But then they all stared in amazement at Sir Bors. Merlin's magic liquid had dripped onto his hand. Slowly, the knight's hand was growing bigger and bigger before their very eyes.

"That'll teach you not to snatch," said the Queen, finishing her chapter and returning to the action.

But Bors was delighted. He raised his enormous mitt into the air and made a gorilla-sized fist. It looked like he lost a hand-shaking contest to a hammer-head shark, who had glomped down on his knuckles.

"Brothers, I have been blessed. From now on, they will call me Knight of the Hammer Hand!" he declared. "And with my mighty fist I will smite down the enemies of Camelot." Bors then put his hand through his bedside table sending flowers everywhere.

"Lucky!" said Sir Gawain, green with envy.

"About time too!" said Guinevere. "Now get out there and defend my honour. You can start by bashing those four idiots who insulted my honour to begin with."

The Head Healer emerged from under a hospital bed. "Is it over?" he asked nervously.

"Not by a long shot," snarked Guinevere. "Not until every king in the land not named Arthur regrets the day they ever crossed me. Form a queue, boys!"

But the knights were not paying attention. They were still trying to grab medicines from Merlin's bag while she was talking

"One at a time!" called the Head Healer in a desperate voice, but it was no use.

"Sir Bors!" ordered the queen. "Teach them to share."

The knight shoved the others aside with one sweep of his unbelievably large hand and, grabbing Merlin's medicine bag, dropped it near Guinevere's feet. A crowd of sulky knights glared daggers at him, but the fear of getting a bashing from his giant hammer fist kept the mob at bay.

"But your highness," said Sir Losealot. "There's not enough bottles for all of us."

"Good point, good knight. There's only one fair way to do this," said the queen in a voice both firm and sensible. "I will mix up the magic medicine in this bed pan."

She checked it had not been used.

"Then every knight can fill a cup and drink at the generous price of one silver penny per cup."

A massive cheer went up. The knights didn't care for the price. They would pay anything to get their hands on Merlin's magic medicine and instantly formed a queue. Guinevere took a ladle and began sharing out the miracle cure. It was the refreshing colour of purpley brown.

"Are you sure it's a good idea to mix Merlin's spells up?" whispered the Head Healer. Guinevere continued to fill the bed pan regardless and the pile of silver pennies grew larger and larger.

But the queen could not hear his words over the excited chatter of the knights, either that or she chose to ignore him. Either way, in no time at all, every Knight of the Round Table had a small mug of purple-brown liquid to call his own. The green fumes only added to its peculiar flavour.

"I will fight any knight for the honour of being first to ride out of the gate!" cried a familiar voice.

"No you won't Lancelot!" commanded the queen. "You will ride at the back, to protect me. We're not doing this again!" Then she stepped forward and raised her ladle in triumph.

"Knights! Drink your soup and be hearty," she cried. "For now, we ride to Arthur's aid and to the rescue of Camelot!"

The knights let out a loud cheer, downed their drinks in a single gulp, and were violently sick.

Chapter 34
Trial By Kingly Clobbering

"But I wanted an execution!!!" screamed King Arty in a strop."It's not fair! It's not fair! It's not fair!"

The little tyrant was famous for flying into tantrums at the drop of a silk handkerchief. Now he was boiling over into a caldron of rage stew. Stropping about his tent, Arty's face had turned the special sort of red you only see on deadly toadstools or smashed up watermelons.

Arthur and Merlin waited patiently outside. They had been thrown in a pit (which was a little like a jail cell but with better views of the birds). In each corner was a large gate. Behind the gates were the sound of growling coming from something sinister blanketed in shadow. With a running jump, you might be able to climb it's chipped walls if you were quick with your hands and feet. But, surrounded by many soldiers looking down on them, it was unlikely the king or wizard were even thinking of escaping.

Despite Arty's performance, King Oither (the Obvious) refused to budge. He had spent most of the morning consulting a very heavy book called 'The What, Where, When, and Why of War'. Currently he was thumbing a section about what to do when your enemy king turns up without an army. Here, there weren't many words of advice as the authors clearly thought no king would ever be this dumb. Still they wrote a few sentences about the best way to get a fair result so that nobody would lose any honour.

Finishing the last sentence, Oither had his answer. Being such a matter of fact kind of man, facts kind of mattered to him. One snotty tot's shouting was not going to change his mind. Rules were rules and had to be followed. In fact, he considered moving Arty's bed time to four in the afternoon.

"There," said Oither. "I've sentenced him to trial by combat. That way, everything is nice and by the book." He stamped a document with his royal seal (It was a badger losing a card game to a team of rabbits).

"Sign Mr wizard up too," added Halfer. "I'm still missing

my special silver spoons."

"Rats!" grumbled Merlin, hoping they'd forgotten about his sticky fingers.

"Very well," said Oither. "Two for combat to the death. No ifs, ands, or buts."

The kings shifted their thrones overlooking the pit. On the front row, they had the best view in the entire army of Arthur's demise. But neither Arthur nor Merlin seemed all that bothered by their fate. Both were passing time by playing a game of "I Spy". Merlin had chosen 'D' and Arthur had correctly guessed 'Dork' pointing to Oither.

"Any last words?" Little king Arty gave a big, evil laugh. He would grow up into a fine villain.

"Hmm... not much faith in my fighting skills, I see." Arthur thought for a second. "How about… Get lost Young Poop!" Then he and Merlin gave out full-bellied laughs and rolled around on the floor near puddles of something red.

"It's Young Pup not Young Poop!" hissed Arty in a rage. "He can't have that for his last words!"

"Ha! Young Poop. It's the punning of your English." Arteur hadn't said a line for a while. "Those are some last words, tres amusant! It's funny, non?"

"Come on, kings!" said Arthur with a comedy shrug. "I have no champion. I'm a ruler not a fighter." The king then growled like a hungry kitten and tucked in his fingers to make a paw.

"Of course, by the rules of the book, you have the right to choose a champion," said Oither flicking through a few pages. "Have you any champions or significant others ready to fight for you?"

"Merlin, old buddy, old pal," said Arthur playfully. "Do you happen to know any champions?"

"Me sire? I've got nothing. I'm just a tired old man in a pointy hat and a threadbare bathrobe," said the wizard, idly kicking the dirt.

"What about that old Lanceylot fellow? Good in a scrape I hear." Arthur picked up a sword hanging from the wall. He tutted and put it back.

"Him?" scoffed Merlin. "Wouldn't trust him to mow the lawn." The wizard examined a hefty axe and casually dropped it on the floor.

"I hear good things about those Rotund Table gentlemen. Maybe they can help?" The king let out a casual burp.

"Oh no, no, no," tutted Merlin. "Not in a million years, sire. They spend so much time around tables they'll probably give you splinters." He yawned and rubbed a bored eye.

"Stop stalling and get on with it!" yelled Oifer.

"Yeah, stop wasting our time," shouted Arty.

"I came here to see you gentlemen sliced like fine steak," added Arteur as he peeled some vegetables for supper.

"OK. Good point, good point." said Arthur. He waved his hands as a sign of peace. "Oh well, that's enough sarcasm. Merlin and I aren't afraid. Not of you. We don't need a champion. We'll stomp you into the dust right here, right now. Bring on your biggest grunt, you fearsome foursome!"

The enemy army were struck dumb. This Arthur was very different from the chicken everyone knew and avoided. The kings looked at each other and nodded. He was probably bluffing. With his pudgy little gut and lack of muscles, he had to be bluffing.

"Ha!" said Halfer in a voice that was half a laugh and half a grunt. "Enough of the hero chat. Let the games begin!"

There was a fanfare of trumpets and evil cheering from the many enemy soldiers. They were all hungry for the smushing. Down in the pit, a gate opened and a dark shadow bumped its head on the roof. Through the smoke strode an enormous figure into the arena. Standing straight, he was bigger than three houses and wider than twelve pigs.

"Meet Gawr the Giant!" sneered Arty. "The Beast of Brittany!"

"The same Gawr who eats three whole cows for lunch?" asked Merlin. "Not impressed."

"Yes and he'll have your king for breakfast!" crowed Halfer.

"Hey! That's not nice!" said Arthur. "There's not enough calories in me to give a giant a light snack."

"Me Gawr!" boomed the giant. "Meet skull smasher!"

The giant's great oak club reminded Arthur of a huge leg of roast beef but it was peppered with steel spikes. The giant raised his club effortlessly with a flick of a tree trunk sized wrist and saluted the kings.

"Hi Gawr. Me Arthur. Him Merlin," said Arthur without a

trace of fear. "May best man win!"

"Me Win!" boasted the giant. "Skull Smasher smash you!"

"A skull smasher did you say?" said Arthur, stalling for time. "Could I use it as a back scratcher?"

The ground shook as the giant stomped towards the king. Now he was really offended. Arthur yawned and stretched, not caring about the danger. Already, he was planning his victory parade.

"Sire, I think it's about time we got on with the plan," whispered the wizard, giving Arthur a gentle prod.

"Very well," grumbled Arthur, rather enjoying the show. "Merlin, if you've got anything up your sleeve, now would be a good time to produce it."

"Ah ha!" cried Merlin, producing two glowing bottles from his sleeve. Both shone in bright white light. If you listened close enough, angels started to sing.

"Excalibur be praised!" said Arthur. He slapped both hands on his cheeks in mock surprise. "Could it possibly be the Lancelot spell? Merlin, may I?" The king's sarcasm had crossed the line into being smug.

"Of course, sire," said the wizard. "Down the hatch!"

Merlin passed a glowing glass bottle into the King's outstretched hand as the giant closed the gap between them in two mighty strides. Arthur opened it and drank the liquid inside with one gulp. With a wild swing of his powerful arm, Gawr swung Skull Smasher with every inch of his might. The club whipped round in the blink of an eye and slammed down heavily on Arthur's head. But, instead of the book ending here, the giant's weapon harmlessly bounced off the king's face.

There was a shocked silence. Gawr clubbed Arthur again and again, but the result was the same. There wasn't even an eyebrow out of place on Arthur's chops. The giant gave a confused look (since his face always looked confused, he now looked very stupid). Skull Smasher had hit its mark, but there was no splatter.

Gawr would quickly learn that Merlin's Lancelot spell gives a person incredible strength and keeps them safe from any harm. Last night, Arthur and Merlin had finally found a useful potion and came up with a scheme to stack the deck in their favour (which was lucky because they were running out of rats). Later, Lard the Jailer would find a rat-shaped hole in their cell wall where the rodent had smashed his way to freedom. That rat's escape proved to Arthur and Merlin they had finally found the Lancelot spell.

"Mind if I have a turn?" asked Arthur with a grin. Then he took Gawr by his big toe and began to twirl the giant around as if he was as lighter than a pillow. The giant was slammed to the floor, lifted up in the air, and returned to the familiar floor once more. Arthur repeated this process until the giant was very dizzy and hurt indeed. To the enemy, it seemed like the king was using Gawr like a sledgehammer looking for a missing tent peg. Then Merlin joined in the fun. Soon he and Arthur threw the giant back and forth like a beefy beachball. Gawr begged for mercy but he was drowned out by the booing of a very upset audience.

"Hey! They're cheating!" wailed Arty. He was preparing himself for another tantrum.

"Does that mean we can go home now?" asked Merlin. He nearly dropped Gawr, but caught him just in time, before swatting him back to Arthur.

"Non! You are not playing fair!" said Arteur. "Oither, mon ami, this cannot be allowed to continue, non?"

Oither thought for a second and stood up from his chair. "Hmmm. What say you, referee witches?"

Three green hags dressed in black and white stripes looked at one another. Then they formed a huddle and began to whisper in secret. Moments later, the head witch stepped forward.

"Penalty! Using illegal spells!" she declared as the crowd cheered. All three witches zapped Arthur and Merlin with black lightning from their fingertips, robbing the two of their magical strength. The Lancelot potion had just been cancelled.

"Let's try again," mumbled Oither, returning to his seat. Arthur and Merlin were left weaker than a new-born caterpillar. The king tried to dig a hole in the ground to his freedom. Merlin strained his little finger trying to lift a sword from the pit wall. Forced to play fair, the duo dropped their cocky act. Now they would certainly meet their doom at the hands of Gawr.

Just then a voice cried out: "Wait!"

"Finally, some good luck at last," said Arthur. "Does this schtick ever end?"

"My minstrel, Sid the Singer, wants to hear your last words," explained young Arty. "He's gonna make up a brand new song to celebrate your death. What have you got for us this time, Sid?"

A bald headed minstrel stepped forward strumming a battered harp. Raising his arms in the sky, he soon got the entire enemy army clapping to the beat. As a rhythm section, they weren't bad. After turning Camelot to rubble, they might go on tour as a travelling band.

He's got a big nose. He's got a big head
That fool of a king will soon be dead
He's Arthur… Dead Arthur…

He wouldn't be beat. He wouldn't compete.
That fool of a king used magic to cheat.
He's Arthur… Dead Arthur

So not such a smarty. He's probably farty.
That fool of a king throws a bad birthday party
He's Arthur… Dead Arthur...

And Here is his end. He's no longer a friend.
That fool of a king drives you straight round the bend
He's Arthur… Dead Arthur...

The audience took up the chorus of 'Dead Arthur" and swooshed their axes around. Playing to a home crowd, Gawr returned to his feet and grinned. Arthur whimpered. The giant took Skull Smasher and started making holes in the pit floor.

Meanwhile, both king and wizard started running in circles, wailing, totally terrified. Arthur knew his death was not going to be pleasant. Skull Smasher was the perfect weapon for turning a king's brain to porridge.

Chapter 35
Halftime Refreshments

Queen Guinevere rode on horseback toward the enemy camp. This time she had company. In her mind, she half wanted to rescue Arthur. The other half wished to rain down painful revenge on those kings who thought she wasn't queen-material. Lancelot was at her side on a horse with anger management problems. His horse was very useful in a scrape, but it was banned from victory parades.

"My lady, shouldn't we be going toward the action?" asked Lancelot. "I hear there's some men-at-arms who could use a manly whiffing." It had been many pages since Lancelot had used his sword, Aroundight. This was the legendary sword that had a name that sounded like a brand of washing up liquid. Still, Camelot's greatest knight was hungry for the fight.

"In good time, Lancelot," pronounced the queen,"there's enough baddies for all of you to give a pasting."

This was met with a deep, croaky, all-male hurrah!

The Knights of the Round Table followed behind her. Their recovery had not been pretty. In fact, a couple of cups of Guinevere's magic mixture had actually made them feel worse before they got any better. To those who remembered, the potions in the bed pan tasted like a banana-parsley-moss-pork-strawberry-dung-mustard-soup crossed with a minty-baked-bean-cottage-cheesy-BBQ-radish flavour with a sour aftertaste of toothpaste-wholegrain-chili-powder-tea-scented-goat. Most got their eyesight back inside a few hours and, once they stopped being pot-bellied pigs, had healed rather quickly.

Only Sir Tristan showed any sign of his former injuries. He had sore knees. Many of the knights suspected he had given his third cup to some unlucky pot plant. It was an important lesson to never mix unlabeled potions again which they would quickly forget by the time of the next jousting tournament.

"We'll be there soon enough," chuffed the queen. "Right after a spot of cake."

Through the morning fog, she caught sight of a small rickety shack crowned by a cardboard cupcake. Guinevere ordered the knights to halt. When the queen came closer, the mists began to part, revealing a refreshment cart and Morgana Le Fey in a white apron. The sign above her cart read "The Gingerbread Witch" while a slightly smaller sign read "Broken biscuits – Half Price!"

"So the Gingered bread witch walks among us," said Guinevere. "I thought she was a made-up character for adverts... like Candy Dan the Garlic Man, or Molly the Filthy Mop, or Willford the Dragon Sandwich Dragon."

"Nope! she's as real as you and I," said Morgana flashing her logos. "And thanks to your stupid husband, the Gingerbread Witch is homeless and looking to secure some quick cash." She pushed a tray of tasty treats underneath the queen's nose. "Biscuit?"

"What are you really doing here, foul conjuror?" wondered Sir Gawain out loud. "Evil magic, I bet."

"Causing trouble, I suspect," added Sir Bors.

"Plotting our doom, I expect," offered Sir Headstrong.

"Selling cursed charms, I have no doubt," said Sir Percival. He squinted hard at a cardboard cut out of a gingerbread man. Not even its gumdrop smile would give it the benefit of the doubt.

There was not a knight in Camelot who trusted Morgana and for good reason. The last time she came to the kingdom, they found themselves taking arms up against their own pyjamas.

"Sir knights, I come in peace," said the witch with a wide toothy grin on her face. "Not to mention I come with the latest release from the Gingerbread Witch Bakery," Morgana trotted over to a foldaway table and pulled back a specially placed checkered cloth, "Presenting... Morgana's special gingerbread!"

There were plates and plates of gingerbread biscuits. They gave off a spicy, nutty smell that was pleasing to the nose. Each was decorated with a curious green icing and sprinkled with leafy chunks. Every gingerbread cookie looked good enough to eat as the knights' hands began to tremble, eager to grab one and scoff it down.

"I want to give one to everyone in Camelot," added Morgana. "Free of charge, of course!"

"Special gingered bread! I say!" cried Sir Galahad, handing over a coin and grabbing a handful of reddy bread without a second thought. "I have heard many tales of this finest of breads. Pray, what is the secret ingredient?"

"Gingerbread!... and nothing else!" Morgana yelled. Every head in a helmet raised a concerned eyebrow and stopped nibbling.

"What's the catch?" asked Sir Cador with deep mistrust.

"Don't ask! I will never reveal my secret," added the witch. "If I ever blabbed, I'd have to turn all of you into toads."

"And…" began Guinevere. "What if I were to remind you that I am queen around here, and people who don't tell me the truth fast are thrown in the castle moat. Here, in Camelot, we don't keep secrets." Sir Lancelot was about to open his mouth, but was quickly shushed.

To help Morgana with her honesty, the Knights of the Round Table had their swords ready and pointed at her head.

"Alright! Alright!" confessed the witch. "Just because I'm here selling my wares doesn't mean I'm not out for a little revenge. Come on! Your stupid king destroyed my home after all!"

"I'm sure he did…" said Guinevere. She didn't need any evidence. The sky was blue, water was wet, and Arthur ruined lives. "But if I allowed everyone who Arthur annoyed to destroy the kingdom, I'd be queen of a small hill of rubble."

"Curses!" cursed the witch.

"As for that secret recipe..." asked Guinevere coyly as she sniffed different biscuits, "it wouldn't happen to be a certain weed, would it?"

"Any more talk like that and you'll get such a toading!" threatened Morgana.

"It is cluckawort!" yelped Sir Galahad on his fifth special biscuit. Thankfully, he'd never worked a day in his life and would be spared the dreadful side-effects.

"Cluckawort!" sighed the queen. "Morgana, I am disappointed. You're really losing your touch as a wicked witch. I remember a time when a terror like you would strike real fear into Camelot. You would rain screaming skulls on us and turn all our cobblestones into zombies. Now look at you, hoping to trick us with baked goods. Merlin does more damage to the kingdom on fireworks night."

"I know!" wailed the witch. "Ever since I lost my home, I've been all out of ideas." She crouched down and rocked back and forth. "Help me, Guinevere. I'm trapped in a rut of cakes and failure."

Guinevere hopped off her horse and knelt near the witch. She leant in close to the witch's ear.

"Morgana, what would you say to enough gold to buy three castles and a bigger cauldron?"

Morgana's eyes lit up. The witch didn't know it yet, but she actually yelled out. "Cha-ching!"

Unfortunately, a bad thing happened while they weren't keeping an eye on their surroundings.

"Ha! Ha! Ha! Look who we've got here," chuckled a wicked captain. "A damsel in distress and her tins of sardines." By the look of his pitch black armour and devil horns, he was definitely not from Camelot.

Neither was the large group of fighting men accompanying him. There were knights on elephant-back. Behind them were men at arms with many arms, standing grimly to attention. A dwarf regiments from Halfer's group were there too, armed with spiked axes. Joining them were lines of French crossbowmen, the handpicked elite of King Arteur. On their tunics they wore the proud badge of Camembert – a white chunk of runny cheese – and armed with the famous Cumbrian iron studded clubs. For a scouting party, it was a little excessive, but the four kings had more than enough troops to spare. Now, they had caught the queen and her knights snacking.

"Lancelot! Lancelot! Set me free, you know you want to. It'll be fun! Bwa-ha-ha!" The voice was Aroundight. Lancelot's sword with a name that sounded like a pair of tights designed for fatter legs. The star knight was so hungry for battle he thought he was hearing things. He quickly shook his head and tried to focus.

"I see we have been ambushed," said Guinevere.

Yes, they had dear reader.

"Duh!" replied Morgana unhelpfully.

The scout captain pointed his sword at them and gave a wicked smile.

"Somebody had to make sure you Camelot folk didn't get the drop on us," he said, laughing with the men. "But

I didn't think we'd ever bag the top prize." The evil villain stared at Guinevere. With this capture, he could retire to the countryside and join the local tennis team.

The Knights of the Roundtable closed ranks around their queen. Even with Lancelot going a little crazy, this was a fight they couldn't win. The captain trotted back and forth, continuing to ramble on. He addressed the scouting unit, adding his own evil laugh here and there.

"Boys, the others might be back at camp watching that idiot Arthur lose a duel to a giant! But it looks like we'll have to make do with our own entertainment."

Slowly, the over-sized scouting unit of hundreds slowly crept toward our doomed heroes.

"Aww. I never got a chance to start smiting." Sir Gawain was Sir Glum.

"Aww! I never got the chance to run away!" Sir Gahalad wished he was Sir Gone.

"It's not too late, Lancelot," whispered Aroundight, a sword with a name that sounded like a diet of eating round things.

"Quiet you!" replied the best knight. He wasn't crazy no matter how much his sword talked.

Just then, Morgana stepped forward and yelled "You don't scare me! I'm the Gingerbread Witch!" She wasn't bluffing and acted as if she owned all the aces in a deck of cards.

"What's the plan, witch?" asked Guinevere, still unsure whose side Morgana was on.

"Two words, your highness," said Morgana. "Enchanted eggs!"

"Enchanted eggs!" shouted everyone. All were confused.

"Enchanted eggs," said the witch. "I keep a cart full of birds behind the stall. You never know when you might need eggs to make gingerbread mix."

"Enchanted eggs! What nonsense!" scoffed Lancelot. "For that, you'd need magical hens!"

"I never said hens," said Morgana. "I've got pheasants. Much better eggs!"

At that, Morgana grabbed her plates of special gingerbread biscuits and threw them over her refreshment cart roof. And, as if to prove the truth of the witch's words, a loud clucking broke out behind the wheeled shack. It was higher in pitch than the cluck of a hen and the clucks came in matched pairs – cluck cluck – cluck cluck. They were only getting louder.

"The birds sound riled up," said Sir Tristan. "I wonder what's spooked them?" He rubbed his knee which ached.

Guinevere peered behind the cart. The loud double clucks turned into a roaring stream of frenzied squawking. There was a frightful flapping noise followed by a crash. Their cage had been torn open. The queen's eyes widened as she saw hundreds and hundreds of pheasants going off their rockers. The birds were mad and looking for something to peck.

"Take cover!" Guinevere screamed.

"CLUCKAWORT!!!!"

The pheasants charged the scouting party and, in no time at all, the swarms of feathers had sent them packing. The frightened men retreated across the plains as every bird hunted them endlessly. Being pecked and clawed from all sides, and 'clucks' ringing in their ears, the scouts pulled back to their main camp. But the mad pheasants followed. With a good eye, Guinevere and her knights could see the enemy camp turned upside down with crazy birds. They heard the distant screams and shouts of many millions taken by complete surprise. Soon, everything was in complete chaos.

"Well that was lucky," chirped Guinevere. The foul fowl have done most of our work for us."

While they sat about and laughed at their unlikely win, they heard the distant sound of exploding thunder. Something shot past them at lightning speed, sending them falling from their horses. Stunned into silence, the group were very confused (as if the day could get any more confusing.) Whatever the thing was, it left behind a faint limey glow and the mild smell of pine.

Guinevere got back to her feet and dusted herself down.

"Did we forget anyone?" she asked.

Chapter 36
Of Feathers and Fear

No more than an arrow's shot away (if shot from a strong arm and with a good wind. Let's say it was just under a mile), King Arthur and Merlin were fighting for their lives against Gawr the Giant. 'Fighting' was a generous word. More like they were running and hiding with the best of intentions. The giant had not forgiven their 'Lancelot Spell' stunt and was out for blood.

"Arrrgggghhhh!" bellowed Gawr. It was something giants normally said when swinging a club. He gave another swing from Skull Smasher as Arthur hurled himself out the way. Its evil iron spikes bit into the ground, spewing up clouds of dirt. With little effort, the giant prised his weapon from the mud. With his poor aim, the giant had left holes and bunkers all over the pit. The arena looked like the world's most dangerous golf course. But, finally, he had cornered the king.

Arthur cowered in a bunker left by one of the giant's previous misses. It wasn't very kingly to jump into a muddy hole, and hop into a muddy hole, and hide in another muddy hole, but Arthur was out of options. His choices had been to scurry around like a cowardly rabbit or stand there and get squished.

He looked for Merlin, but true to form, the wily wizard had disappeared and was nowhere to be found. Arthur wondered in which hole he was hiding. Unfortunately, the king had just run out of hiding holes. Gawr had him trapped with nowhere else to run. Closing his eyes, Arthur waited for the fatal blow and thought about the many silly things that had led him here.

Suddenly there was the most dreadful cockadoodledoo. A great shadow fell that smelt faintly of eggs and herbs upon the forces of the allied kings. It was followed by the vexed clucking of countless high-pitched birds. The air was suddenly thick with feathers and fear.

"Qu'est que le heck!" blurted out Arteur. He was right to be shocked.

"What are those things?" shouted Halfer. "I've never seen a

bird act so wild."

"Bad birds!" squealed Arty.

"Abandon duel!" yelled Oither leaping from his throne. The other three kings soon joined him, followed by every soldier, knight and heavy grunt not in direct combat with a crazed pheasant. They all turned heel and ran for safety, no matter how far away it seemed. Soon the weed-maddened birds had completely overrun the enemy camp and sent them fleeing.

Amongst the pecks of chaos came a clear and mighty shout. A limey flash shot toward Arthur, accompanied by a trademark hearty "Ha, ha, ha, ha!". The king's heart beat like a bongo in a samba band and sat down to recover his senses.

"Hands off him, you!" cried the figure, unsheathing his olive axe. "Pick on someone your own bloomin' size!"

Arthur was dizzy from playing 'whack a mole' with Gawr. "Is that you Lancelot?" he mumbled before collapsing into the hero's tree trunk arms like an unsent package.

"No!" boomed the voice. "It is I, The Green Knight and none other! And now I am all pruned out!"

"Gruh?" demanded Gawr.

"I am he! The great Green Knight is…, uh I." said the Green Knight. "Now face my minty fury!"

"Me no see you! Show you now!" roared Gawr. The giant stamped his feet but was unable to find his opponent. Even though the Green Knight in all his greenness stood out like a sore thumb against the brown muck found in the pit, still Gawr kept missing and leaving more holes in the floor. The reason soon became obvious. Gawr the Giant was colourblind (giants often are). And the Green Knight was green (green knights often are). So, to Gawr, Ol' Greeny was invisible.

"I'm standing right here in front of you," huffed the Green Knight. He was growing tired of this nonsense.

"Die!" roared a big mouth belonging to Gawr. The giant charged at him blindly.

"Not today!" replied the green man. "Have at you!"

In a flash, the Green Knight was poking and prodding the unfortunate Gawr. Every jab from his axe irritated the giant who, because of his vision problems, thought his ankles were being attacked by an invisible swarm of bees. The knight's axe couldn't reach much higher. So Ol' Greeny planned to continue hacking at his opponent's shins and somehow work upwards from there.

With the pure thickness of Gawr (in both brain and body), defeating him would take weeks. But the giant was so spooked that he soon took flight. Climbing out the pit, Gawr ran for the hills with his huge strides, leaving comet-sized craters in Camelot's fields. Terry Cotter would later make up tall tales about them for his next tourist attraction.

"You did it, Ol' Greeny!" cheered Arthur, giving his best friend a kingly hug.

"I'd better get after him," replied the Green Knight. "Giants are sore losers. We can't have him rampaging around your lands. Ha, ha, ha, ha."

"Oh no you don't," said the king. "First things first, you'll take me home to Camelot where people aren't trying to slice me into sausages. There, I'll send my guards and accountants away and you'll have unlimited access to the kingdom's treasury… for ten minutes."

"Thank you, sire," said the knight of many greens. "Only if my good friend will join me in a money fight."

"It's a deal," said the king. At that, Arthur jumped on the back of the Green Knight's horse and the two best buds galloped off to Camelot.

"Thank you, Ol' Greeny!" said Arthur. "I am forever in your debt. From this day forward, all school children in Camelot will be forced to eat their greens, in your honour."

For once, things were beginning to look up for Arthur and his kingdom. He'd been rescued. His enemies were having trouble. He would not be fighting a killer giant to the death. Soon, he would finally have his dinner. It was a shame they forgot all about Merlin.

"Where are you going?!" yelled the wizard as Arthur and Ol' Greeny took off beyond the horizon.

Seeing he was by himself, all Merlin could think to say was "rats!" At best, he would have to walk many miles on the road to home.

But then the wizard caught sight of something shivering beneath an overturned throne and went over to investigate. The shivering came from little king Arty and he had had all the trouble he could handle. Merlin gave him a soft smile.

"Greetings young man," he said. "What do you say to winning the silver medal?"

Chapter 37
Your Turn, Lancelot!

All across the battlefield, the forces of Camelot were winning with the help of their 'pheasant allies'. Wherever Guinevere looked, crazed birds were clawing, poking, biting, and causing untold trouble. A giant wave of beaks and feathers covered the countryside and had all but won the day. What was worse for the foe, any peasants among their ranks were now frothing at the mouth and had sided with the pheasants. Anyone not crazy from Cluckawort was now fleeing the scene like rats from a sinking boat (with armbands and life jackets).

Guinevere smirked as she saw Morgana take to the field. She was stealing people's shoes for her newest spell. The woman was a witch reborn and was cackling with glee at thoughts of her future mischief. Without a doubt, Camelot would be hearing from her again. She would probably ride in on a thunder cloud, raining down exploding pumpkins on the poor townsfolk. But, for now, she was a friend.

The queen turned to her knights. "Look boys! Victory is near!" she said, pointing the way forward. "Shouldn't you be off smiting them or something? I'm not having the history books say we won and it was all thanks to birds."

Lancelot shook his head. "I am a knight of the Round Table," he explained. "There's not much honour in bashing a few runaway peasants. I save my steel for real knights."

"Aw. Don't be like that, Lancey," muttered Aroundight. A sword with a name that sounded like a brand of paint for garden fences.

"Hush," whispered the knight.

Guinevere was disappointed. "As you wish Sir Lancelot," she said. "Anyone else have a problem?"

But before she had finished speaking, every knight of the Round Table (except Lancelot) was charging. They yelled "no" when they were already halfway down the hill. Whatever glory Lancelot didn't want, they would happily take.

"Camelot! Camelot!" they cried. At first Guinevere admired this clever little battle plan, but when she saw Sir Lid-shut leading the charge, she realised their mistake. Trapped in his helmet, he couldn't see a thing. Thankfully not everybody ended up in a lake the same way he did.

"Hey! Wait for me!" cried Lancelot, changing his mind. He sprang onto his horse, keen to join in the fun. But Guinevere grabbed him by the greaves and stopped his charge.

"If I'm not mistaken..." said the queen. "Isn't that King Oither over there? You can't miss him. His helmet has a golden crown and he looks like a walking-talking metal palm tree." She pointed across the field to a hill where the king was fighting off angry birds. His full suit of armour had already been dented by peck marks.

Between Lancelot and Oither were the finest knights in the Cumbrian army. They stood in formation, their flags of many colourful owls blowing in the wind. Their war horses snorted fiercely through the nose. They raised their lances high, the steel tips gleamed in the sunlight. Their armour was thick, their accents were thicker. They clearly meant business.

"Eeeee!" Lancelot squealed. An early Christmas present appeared before him.

"Charge over there, please!" called Guinevere. "Go out and bag me an ungrateful king." Keen to get her revenge, the queen gave Lancelot a sharp poke in the ribs and his horse (with the temper troubles) sprinted out to the battlefield.

In the thick of the fighting, Camelot's star knight galloped past many battlefield distractions. A menacing figure clad in black spikes looked like a good challenge. A team of goblins would make an excellent handbag if he had the time. A fiery red dragon was tempting and would be an entertaining story at the tavern later. But none of them were a 'king'. Lancelot wanted the grand prize. He would only slow down if his target had a crown (and only for a few seconds).

The handsome knight sprinted full pelt on his horse. The angry beast carried his rider across muddy ground with ease and bit anyone who was close enough. With hooves louder than thunder, he broke through the enemy lines, knocking soldiers and magical creatures out the way. By the time he reached the wall of Oither's knights, Lancelot quickly added to the hospital beds by fiercely swinging around Aroundight – a sword with a name that sounded like trouble for the Cumbrians. Soon, there was not a knight from the north who hadn't met Lancelot personally and did not regret it.

With a little time to rest, Lancelot saw the other knights of the Round Table having much fun across the battlefield. Remembering fondly all the times he had beaten them up, the knight was happy to see them win for a change. He looked up the hill to where Oither was trying to defend himself.

"Come horse," said Lancelot. He found swords easier to name than animals. "Let us… go up… to get the king!" Sometimes he was a little slow on good speeches too.

Lancelot heard a wet squish, but didn't pay it any mind. He rode ever onward. His mind never left the mission. What the knight didn't know was he had accidentally trampled King Halfer (who due to his short size, Lancelot had not spotted). The dwarf king and his pixie friends were stomped into the dust without Camelot's knight even realizing. Halfer had hoped to make a heroic last stand, but would later be chipped off a horseshoe and sent home in a children's hospital playset.

Meanwhile, away from the mud and sweat, Guinevere spotted something strange going on. "What in the name of Camelot is happening to that donkey?" she wondered out loud. Across the way the beast of burden slowly trotted away from the fighting. He had two figures with him disguised as cup bearers in orange and green uniforms. One had a long white beard. The other was only a snotty boy. They looked like cowardly carrots. The queen swore one of them was Merlin, but couldn't put her finger on which one. Whoever these weirdos were, they were leading the donkey and his large cart toward Camelot castle and arguing like ducks over the last piece of wet bread.

Chapter 38
Aroundight: The Sword With a Name...

After his angry steed left piles of the injured behind him, Lancelot had reached the exact centre point of the battle. There was hardly a scratch on the knight yet he'd given a dozen or more unlucky enemies a thorough bashing. Truly, no enemy could withstand him (as the songs say). After this battle, Lancelot would try and negotiate his own tapestry with the big wigs in knitting. Maybe a full feature length shroud. The choices were limitless.

Raising his visor, Lancelot scanned the crowds for anyone wearing a helmet with a big golden crown or something stupid like that. Sure enough, standing behind a line of oak trees, he found King Oither surrounded by his handpicked bodyguards. They were the finest fighters Cumbira had to offer, the best of the best. Being from a district of lakes, their hair was wet and they looked like they had a good swim before the battle. At a count, there were at least a hundred wet-look warriors for Lancelot to play with.

Eager for more fighting, the handsome knight jumped off his horse mid-charge (briefly outrunning him) and sprinted toward the startled enemy. Lancelot drew his sword and waved it wildly.

"Aroundight!" he cried in challenge. "My sword with a name that sounds like a garlic cheese from Germany!" Deep in his heart, Lancelot agreed with the authors. His sword had a ridiculous name and it pained him to admit it.

"You what?" called King Oither, rather confused.

"I said Aroundight!" called Lancelot again "It's the name of my sword. My sword with a name that sounds like a forward-thinking bank. Dang it!" The knight snapped back to the story once more.

Like a true hero of pure heroics, Lancelot raised his weapon high in the air and stared down his enemies. He gave the sword a spin for good measure and carved a nearby rock into a small statue of him defeating them all.

"Fine," said Oither with a patient smile. "Glad we got that cleared up." He turned to his bodyguard. "Men!" cried the Cumbrian king. "Kill him!"

"Oh! Like hiffle, you will!" bellowed Lancelot, beating his sword into the helmet of the nearest bodyguard and almost splitting it like bread. The man dropped like a felled oak. Many others fell like various trees. One whirlwind of steel later, Lancelot faced Oither alone and man to man.

The dour king held up his sword and ran his finger down the blade to test its sharpness (giving himself a sore pinkie). But when Lancelot took a step toward him with the mad light of battle in his eyes, Oither quickly had second thoughts. Instead of clashing irons, he threw his weapon to the ground and fled the field (he tripped over a few of his bodyguards along the way out).

"Do you yield?" cried Lancelot. Not sure if the king was close enough to hear him.

"I yield! I yield!" moaned Oither, who was running away and yielding at the same time.

Lancelot simply smiled. With this victory, his record for kings defeated had risen to 42, but he had long lost count of defeated knights, dragons, lawsuits, and giants.

Just then, a speedy green dash skidded to a halt and a small, tubby man got off.

"Thank you, Ol' Greeny. I want to see how this one ends," said someone kingly. The green dash took off again leaving his passenger behind. "Of course, Lancelot won," he said. "Wait, when did he get out of the hospital?" Lancelot couldn't believe his eyes. Even though nobody had heard anything of the king for some time, Arthur seemed happy, healthy, and a little short of details about what was going on.

On seeing his king alive and in one piece, Lancelot fell dramatically to his knees and wept.

"Sire, you are saved," he said through manly tears.

"Yup," said Arthur. "Well spotted."

"Sire, glorious news! On this day, I, Lancelot, have defeated an enemy king and saved Camelot," The knight knelt down before the king awaiting praise or a pat on the head saying 'well done'.

"Nice," said Arthur. He thought Lancelot should be on his third king by now, but the king was happy to be anywhere a giant wasn't trying to grind his bones to bread.

"Actually, Lancelot... you've defeated two." Sir Gawain rode over to them. "You accidentally trod on King Halfer. That counts as a very short duel." Gawain held up an injured Halfer imprisoned in his lunch box. His cellmates were a ham sandwich and an orange.

"Two kings I have defeated! Count them. Two!" called Lancelot in a proudly loud voice. He was trying to catch the ear of any passing singers or bards. "The singers will sing about my part in today's great deeds. Let the feasting begin!" he added.

A crowd of victorious Camelotians were slowly gathering. Guinevere arrived pleased as a peacock. She had overseen her first battle plan and it was a tremendous success. The knights of the Round Table had enjoyed their fun day out and were slowly returning from their charge. Many peasants and townspeople had also wandered onto the field (hoping it was now clear of cluckawort and bed-tempered birds). A few carried Sir Softpaws on a nice, fluffy kitchen. Even though the cat hadn't done any actual fighting, he had kept spirits up back home. When everyone heard Lancelot say 'feasting', that was a sure-fire way to catch their attention. The free food and drinks would likely be paid for by Arthur, who didn't want to risk a second invasion by being cheap.

"Not so fast my brave knight!" called Arthur wagging a royal finger. "For there are not two but four enemy kings who stood against me. Halfer may be trampled, Oither may have yielded. Still, there can be no feasting until you have given me a Frenchman and a small boy, or I have four shiny crowns to add to my throne."

The crowd let out a sigh of disappointment. Typical Arthur, he really knew how to kill the buzz of victory. Prince Partypooper had struck again. But Lancelot was tireless in his pursuit of complete and total victory. No promise of food and good times would drag him off the battlefield if any enemies were about. The knight climbed on his horse once more (who was biting Gawain's lunchbox trying to get at Halfer. The dwarf king wailed in fear and hid behind the orange).

"I, Lancelot, the best and bravest of your knights, swear that I will not rest until all four kings have been brought to a swift thumping," he called bravely. He was a little disappointed when nobody cheered. “I will chase them to the ends of the earth!” he added loudly. “It’s very far away.”

“I’m tired,” groaned Guinevere, sitting on a nearby stump. “Why don’t you deal with it?”

“You’ll get more cheers when you return,” promised Arthur. These kinds of promises he usually broke.

Chapter 39
The Escape Donkey of Betrayal

"Call yourself a wizard?" sneered King Arty. "You can't even pull a stupid cart out of a stupid hole in the stupid road!" The little stinker was in a foul mood, even by his stinky standards. First his favourite giant had been chased away by some goof in green armour. Then flocks of strange birds appeared out of nowhere and attacked his beautiful army. Finally, the knights of Camelot somehow had gotten out of their hospital beds and led a charge that sent everyone else running for the hills. Now, carrying cartfulls of stolen Camelot gold, his escape donkey was stuck in a ditch and some inept wizard was struggling to pull him free. This latest team-up had turned out to be a massive bust.

"Roll up your sleeves, Mr Stinky Robe, I haven't got all day," Arty ordered as he tapped his foot impatiently. Merlin gave the donkey another shove, but the beast outwitted him and ducked at the last minute. The wizard slipped and landed in a muddy puddle where the donkey mocked him with a loud laughing 'hee haw'.

"I might have made a mistake," thought the wizard. Then he saw his own muddy reflection in a Camelot gold plate. "Maybe one more try," he said before being hit on the back of the head by a small stone.

"Move it!" yelled Arty. He was the worst child Merlin had ever met (and Merlin had briefly worked as a birthday clown). Arty threw another stone and had picked up a third. The crotchety wizard fixed the young pup with the hard stare that he usually reserved for misbehaving dragons and charity workers.

"My new lord," began Merlin with thick frowning eyebrows. "My exact words were: 'Don't overload this wagon!' and look at what you did!" The wizard pointed to the giant pyramid of golden stuff slowly slipping from the cart. It was bigger than eleven donkeys. Behind them, gold goblets, rings, coins, and many other treasures had already fallen off. They formed a trail of 'sparkly breadcrumbs' so any fool could follow their escape path to the inch without trying very hard.

"Your point being?" demanded Arty.

"Gold is a very heavy metal. There's only so much you can ask of one donkey," muttered the wizard. The crotchety donkey fixed the old wizard with the hard stare that he usually reserved for people who weren't carrying oats.

"You vouched for this donkey. You told me he was the best in the kingdom," countered the young king. "'I always use him for escaping' you said. Those were your exact words." But before the wizard could answer or give the whelp a clip around the ear, there was a loud neigh and the clatter of hooves. No, the donkey hadn't gotten free. Instead an armoured figure on horseback had appeared. He looked big and strong and could probably carry many cartloads of gold.

"You there!" commanded Arty. "Pull this cart out from the mud and I'll reward you handsomely. You can have any gold I don't want." It was a promise Arty gave to anyone who helped him in his time of need. But Arty could never find any gold he didn't want.

Alas for the silly snot, the armoured figure was none other than Lancelot. A few choice blows from the flat side of his sword and some impressive use of rope later and Arty found himself hog-tied at the side of the road.

"Three kings down," laughed Lancelot. "One more to go." He juggled a golden goblet before putting it back (Lancelot had enough trophies back at home).

Just as he was loading Arty onto the back of his horse, Lancelot heard some strange sounds. They were naughty words matched by some annoyed 'hee-hawing'. He turned and saw something trying to flee through the nearby woods. The person of interest was a hunched old man dressed in a sparkling orange and green uniform who was losing an argument to a donkey.

"Merlin?" said Lancelot, raising his visor. "What in the name of grails holy and not are you doing here?"

"Isn't it obvious?" said Merlin without missing a beat."

"No," replied the knight "I have no idea why you're not back at the castle."

"Well…" said the wizard, playing for time. "I'm… I was…

Well, I was rescuing the royal treasure."

Every wizard was fast at conjuring up excuses. That was another one of the things they taught you at wizard school (along with glossing over past failures).

Lancelot raised an eyebrow "How did you know it had gone missing?" In knight school, you were taught how to get to the heart of the matter (and guts of your enemy).

"Wizards know these things, Lancelot," countered the sneaky conjuror. "I wouldn't be of much use to King Arthur, praise his name, and all of Camelot if I couldn't take a glimpse into the future now and then."

The gorgeous knight was almost taken in but instead simply smiled and wagged his finger.

"You almost had me there," he admitted. "Making off with the king's treasure is more like it. But not so fast old man, because I, Lancelot, the most glorious knight in Camelot have caught you with your thieving fingers dipped in the royal treasure chest."

"That's where you're wrong," said Merlin. Then he tried to run away mid-sentence. The wizard ran a few good metres before his donkey finally tripped him up (they were not good friends). In the future, theirs would be a rivalry for the ages.

"You're coming with me wizard," said Lancelot waving his sword about dramatically and slapping some chains on Merlin. "I will escort you back to Camelot myself... just as soon as I get that cart out of the mud."

"Good luck with that," muttered Merlin.

Chapter 40
Nice Guys Finish French

The afternoon slipped into evening as everyone waited for Lancelot to return. By now, there was not an enemy soldier left to be seen. On the hillside, Arthur and Guinevere played back to back games of 'four in a row' to help pass the time. Many Round Table knights watched them with great interest because there was nothing better to do.

"What's keeping Lancelot? He's usually so quick at the mishing and mashing of skulls," wondered Guinevere, out loud. "Also my bishop sinks your battleship. House!" (Neither of them knew the rules to 'four in a row').

"Maybe he's having a spot of bother," said Arthur. He flipped the board over in defeat and picked on one of the knights. "Bors, you'd better go find him."

But the Knights of the Roundtable were restless by now and desperate for another mission.

"Can't I go, sire?" Sir Gawain shot his arm up.

"No, please let it be me?" Sir Losealot joined in.

"No," snapped the king. "I said Bors and Bors it will be." Then he turned to the knight in question. "And don't forget, Bors. Two more kings to go, then it's time for that victory feast, I promised. Be back here in under one hour and I'll pour you a cool glass of King Cola myself."

"Of course, my king," said Sir Bors, poking his tongue out at the other knights. Even though magic had left him and his fist was no longer giant-sized, the knight still had a certain mojo. He rode across the field and everyone watched him shrink to the size of a small dot.

"Lucky," mumbled Sir Gawain.

Moments later, stumbling through some thick forest, Sirs Cador, Pokesalot, Tristan, and Headstrong came pulling Morgana's refreshment cart. The witch sat up front trying to balance a dozen eggs using only magic.

"Woo-wee, I'm starving," said Arthur. His rumbly tummy said pretty much the same. "I think I deserve a quick victory snack before the victory feast and I'm sure Sir Bors will agree with me. What does a king have to do around here to get some gingerbread?"

"Not that you deserve any, tum-tum," snapped Morgana. "My pheasants haven't returned and Guinevere's gold is the only thing keeping me from toading you up. So, King Farter, you're just gonna have to wait. And it will..."

"And it will cost you," interrupted Guinevere. Morgana was like a book she read every year.

"Well, we're also out of sugar," Morgana grumbled.

"Hen's teeth!" cried Guinevere. "How much gold do you want now?"

"No, no!" said Morgana. "I'll just have to make scones rather than gingerbread, if it pleases my lady."

"The queen is not pleased," said Guinevere with a frowny face.

"It will do nicely," said Arthur. "As long as I eat something today."

"Or how about if something eats you, non?" boomed a cackling cackle from the sky.

Suddenly, the wind whipped up and blew the flags from the refreshment cart. At that moment there was a loud roar, a puff of smoke and a terrible blast of fire. Arthur looked up. High above them, dark and dreadful wings beat the air. It was not a fat bat.

"A dragon!" cried Arthur. "Where in the name of Excalibur did that come from?"

"One heck of a pet store!" said the queen, trying to read the beast's collar.

A plume of flame seared into a grassy bank next to the Gingerbread Witch's cart.

"Mind my seating area!" cried Morgana, shaking her fist and trying not to tip her cake mix.

The fiery reptile wheeled around and Arthur caught sight of the rider. It was Arteur. The French king was dressed from head to toe in a suit of golden armour, extra spiky. He looked like a blinged out hedgehog.

"Surrender Arthur!" cried Arteur. "Or my dragon will fry you to a crepe."

Arthur craned his neck to see the fire-breathing monster and the clod who sat on his scaly back. He shook his wimpy fist at the dragon rider as the Knights of the Round Table tried to hide him under Morgana's refreshment cart.

"You wouldn't talk so tough without your dragon!" shouted Arthur, obviously bluffing. "Come down here and say that." But the French king was no coward. He was no idiot, either (unlike some kings).

"Is that so, mon petite Arthur?" he said with a smirk. "In that case, I have a proposition. Something you do for me and I do for you."

"Go on," said Arthur, wanting to hear more.

"You have an army, non? And I have a big dragon, non?" said Arteur, pointing at both things with different arms.

Arthur looked around at his knights, queen, and that witch he made homeless. All were shaking with fear before the gigantic dragon and not much help. "Kind of." He whimpered.

"Well, if you want me to get off my dragon, I want you to fight me by yourself," said Arteur. "No extra help, non?"

Arthur thought about this proposition for a long time. Then he ruined everything by opening his mouth. "Sounds fair," he hoped.

"Terrific!" said the French king with a merry chuckle. "We shall duel and the winner gets le grand prize, non? Camelot!"

With expert control, Arteur landed his dragon. Arthur watched him uncomfortably for he had just sat on some nettles. You had to hand it to the French king, he really knew how to handle the flying terror. The dragon knew it too, and raised its massive head, smoke wisps curling from its nostrils. It gave Arteur a look as if to say, "I am big, scaly and scary. Why don't you put your feet up while I take things from here?" But the proud king wagged his finger as if to say 'No, I'm in charge here. My honour depends on a fair fight.' With a flick of his wrist, the king gave the dragon a signal to take off.

"Off you go!" Arteur said. "And don't fill up on horses again, you'll get a tummy ache, eh?"

The dreadful creature beat its wings and flapped away, but not before swooping down and stealing a herd of cows. With a confused moo, they were gone.

Arteur watched his pet go and quietly tutted to himself. "Oh beef! And now he will no have the room for his supper. That greedy little boy, he never listens to me!"

Arteur sighed and pointed his sword towards Arthur. It was the finest forged steel money could buy. But it was hardly a match for Arthur's legendary blade, Excalibur. Camelot's king rose from the nettle patch, yanked the blade from its scabbard with great effort and accidentally poked himself in the toes.

"Rusty?" asked the French king.

"Never!" said Arthur. "This sword comes from the Lady of the Lake. It's 100 percent waterproof."

"What I mean is that it is you who are the rusty, non? Not the sword?" said Arteur, casually tossing his sword between his left hand and right hand and doing a few tricks. If he wasn't a villain, you'd probably have to applaud his swordcraft. Arthur knew not to show off when it came to swordplay. He was never any good at it. He much preferred hiding behind castle walls and firing his good old bow and arrows. While Arthur was lost in thought, the French king lunged forward and instantly swept past Arthur's defences.

"Last chance to yield, non?" offered Arteur.

"I never yield!" Arthur cried, before adding. "Did I just say that?"

"As you wish, mon ami!" snapped Arteur, advancing with another flurry of slashing blows.

Steel rang on steel, Arthur defended himself as best as he could, but this French fencer was too fast, too strong. With a heavy raking sweep, Arteur slapped the blade right out from Arthur's hand and the force of the blow sent him landing on his butt. Excalibur spun in the air and was hurled towards Morgana's cake stall. There it landed in the witch's cake mixture with a floppy wet 'blut'. Spurts of dough shot everywhere as her mixing bowl was sent flying through the air. The knights put their tongues out, hoping for a chance to catch some free cake mix.

"My batter mix!" cried Morgana. "You cack-handed clod! You've spilled it everywhere!"

With another wet 'blut', the bowl landed on Arthur's head covering him in oozing splatters of thick cake batter. With a swagger, Arteur approached his fallen enemy and casually dipped his finger into the goo.

"Needs more sugar, non?" he said coolly. "You Britons cannot, as you say, bake for toffee."

"It's a scone," countered Arthur, missing the play on words. "Or at least it would have been, if you hadn't ruined it."

Arthur tugged at Excalibur but it was stuck fast in the batter. There was no way to retrieve it. Blinded by dough, all of a sudden he heard a gasp of excitement and a mighty cheer ringing out around him.

"That's more like it," said Arthur. "Finally, a show of support." But nobody was cheering for him.

"Sir Softpaws!" they called at the top of their voices. "Hurrah for Sir Softpaws! Hurrah for our hero cat!"

It was indeed Sir Softpaws. With bravery and loyalty, he stood himself up on Arthur's tummy. Fixing a steely stare on the enemy king, the cat let out a meow of challenge.

"What? I am not afraid of un petite kitten!" sneered Arteur.

Once again, the royal cat let out a warning meow that sent the French king into full-bellied laughter. This was a mistake.

In a split-second, Sir Softpaws took off like a flash toward Arteur. On four paws, he ran towards the man in golden armour. The French king tried to shoo him away with a flick of his sword but the cat was too quick. Seeing his target, Softpaws shot up the king's metal trouser leg and through his gold-plated gusset. In no time at all, the cat was deep inside Arteur's armour, tickling him all over. The French king fell over and burst out in a fit of chuckles.

"Good boy!" cried Arthur in delight. "Let him have it!" He was still trying to pull the bowl from his head.

With his vision blurred by tears of laughter and rolling on the floor helplessly, it was Arteur's turn to fall back. But Sir Softpaws appeared to have a plan and it was being followed to the smallest detail. Another tickle forced the French King into a fit of squealing giggles. Soon Arteur lost control of his sword and it spun from his grasp. As Arthur finally removed the bowl from his head, the French king's sword landed with a cakey splurge, right next to Excalibur. Now both swords were stuck fast.

"Not you as well!" wailed Morgana. "You can forget about scones, my mix is ruined."

Arteur ran over to Arthur and desperately pulled at his sword. He continued to be paralyzed by Sir Softpaws and his tickle attack and flapped his arms in funny directions. Not to be outdone, King Arthur grabbed Excalibur by the hilt and tugged hard, trying to free his legendary blade from the gooey mixture. Both swords were trapped in the bowl with both kings yanking at either end.

"Pull, my lord! Pull!" cried Sir Bors, who was back. Soon the knights took up the chant.

"You can do it, my king!" cried Lancelot, who was also back. "Pull it! Then teach him what we do to invaders!"

"Mhwuph!" exclaimed Arty. Now he was Lancelot's prisoner, it was unclear who he wanted to win.

"What are you all waiting for?" cried an angry voice. It was the Morgana. "Shoot him with arrows! He ruined my scone batter."

"Which one?" asked Guinevere with a raised eyebrow.

"The one wearing the crown," Morgana explained and pointed two hands at Arthur and Arteur.

Guinevere glowered. The witch would be forever disloyal, no matter how much gold she got for an afternoon's work.

Finally Arteur was able to unclasp a golden glove and Sir Softpaws dashed out the opening and ran to Guinevere. The French king was hopping mad. He may have been tickled, but he wasn't laughing now.

"You have broken your word, Arthur," grumbled Arteur. "I wanted we should have a duel with honour, non? But your kitty devil has, as you say, interfered. I said, no, help from your friends."

At that, Arteur produced a small sinister whistle and gave it a good blow. It let out an ear-splitting peep.

"Now, I am the cheater too," Arteur laughed. "My word is also broken, non? Now I do not have a cat up my sleeve, all I have left are my tricks." Then he trailed off into evil laughter.

At that moment, the sky turned black and the ground began to quake. Every Camelotian let out a terrified gasp at what they saw. Dark wings beat the air once more. A thousand feet, hooves, and trotters marched toward them. Warm air circled from the nostrils of many beasts. All were under a spell from King Arteur's whistle and slowly trudged toward Camelot castle. They marched like zombies (except for some zombies who were slightly quicker than before). In one table-turning move, Arteur had all but secured the kingdom's doom. Guinevere covered her eyes as rows of unstoppable scary creatures slowly advanced toward her home, ready to turn its citizens to cinders.

But then, something small yet brave stopped their advance. Across the black grass, missing weapons, and chunks of mud on the battlefield, it strode forward and met the mighty foe head on. Standing strong like a hero in a fluffy orange overcoat was Sir Softpaws. He wasn't scared. He wasn't angry. Instead he walked toward the army of creatures and tried to reason with them.

"Meow!" began Sir Softpaws. "Meow meow, meow meow meow." He took a dramatic pause. "Meow! Meow meow purr hiss meow meow. Meow." Then the cat walked among the crowd, telling them all he had learned in recent days. "Meow meow meow," he recalled, since swallowing Merlin. "Meow meow hiss hiss hiss," he added remembering Arthur's training. "Purr? Purr purr meow purr." Much had happened to one cat. "Meow meow meow meow meow." Spotting a dragon, he placed a paw gently on its talon and looked the creature in the eye with sympathy. "Meow? Meow, meow purr, purr? Meow! Hiss!" Then he climbed on a rocky ledge overlooking them all. "Meow! Meow! Hiss! Purr! Meow! Meow!"

If the authors could speak cat (which they can't, everything above was guesswork), they might have done justice to what was the greatest speech in human history (cat history too). Not a creature was unmoved by the words of Sir Softpaws, except every human there who was confused as heck by the entire display.

Trolls began to tear up. Skeletons swore to change their ways on the spot. There was not a dry eye for any vampires present. Ghouls clutched at their chests. Werewolves threw their arms around each other and wept. Goblins dropped to their knees in awe. Witches and wizards broke their wands and apologized. The sprites and pixies swore oaths of eternal friendship. Even a family of deer (who were nearby but not really part of this) vowed to live better and exercise more often. Every dragon there flew up to the skies and set out on a quest to better understand themselves. Arthur loudly blew his nose and nearly ruined the moment.

Soon, they began to leave, taking the king of Brittany with

them, no matter how much he protested. Arteur was packed up on a flimsy wooden boat and sailed safely back home across the channel waters. Once home, the king told anyone who would listen about how he was defeated by a single cat, but nobody took him seriously. After all, in Brittany they were dog people. They much preferred to hear stories about brave mutts and mighty poodles rescuing children from high places and dangerous farms.

With the battle ended and Camelot safe (until the next disaster), Arthur's whoopsie had finally been undone. Sir Softpaws had become a legend. His last stand had saved them all, and gained many friends in the creature community. Regular folk would no longer remember him as Arthur's cat. From that point on, Arthur would be Sir Softpaws's human. It was also rumoured that the cat would be guest of honour at Captain Funnynuggets's next birthday.

Epilogue

The Tale of Sir Softpaws

"Didn't Sir Softpaws make a most brilliant speech? One for the ages and no mistake," said Merlin with a smile. The wizard was talking to two peasant women in Camelot's town square. Both were huge fans of the royal cat. Everything they owned seemed to have at least one picture of him. Somehow they even smelt like a lot of cats, though none were to be seen.

"You know," the wizard added. "That Softpaws is going places, I tell you. I'd bet my wand on it! I was thinking of becoming his special advisor."

"I know!!! He's so cute!!!" gasped one woman. She clutched a plate celebrating Camelot's recent victory over the enemy. The plate also had a picture of Softpaws. He was wearing a clean white bandage on his little kitty head.

"Hurrah for our hero cat!" called her friend. "He's super brave! We're so happy you like him too."

"Me too. Me too," grinned Merlin. "I'm so glad we're all such good friends."

The wizard tried to stretch out his stiff arms, but they were locked in place by the town stocks.

He'd spent the last few days chained up and snacking on thrown vegetables. This was his punishment for stealing the royal gold and generally being a traitor who couldn't be trusted with an open can of beans. Merlin had accepted his fate with grace (after a bit of haggling over the sentencing). But now his limbs were numb, the crafty conjuror was eager to be free and get started on his next scheme.

"Well… now we're best friends," said Merlin to the women. "How about you loosen these locks a bit? We can go to Camelot Coffee together." He had a dark twinkle in his eye.

"Leave that villain alone!" yelled a deep voice who threw a cabbage at the wizard's nose.

Lancelot was patrolling the busy Camelot streets. Defeating three mighty and menacing kings of Britain, he had been greatly rewarded with a shiny golden suit of armour. Arthur didn't think the Arteur would be needing it anymore. By a miracle, Lancelot and the French king wore the same size breastplate. It was a perfect fit. Now the knight shone so brightly he was invited to stand on the kingdom's cliffs at night and keep lost boats away. He was also given the right to rename Aroundight, the sword with a name that sounded like a brand of face cream. In the end, he settled on the name 'Alan' after his grandmother.

The rest of the Round Table followed behind him. Sir Gawain was dragging around 'Skull Smasher' (Gawr's club was double the knight's height and made a mess of the roads wherever he went). Sir Bors wore three layers of thick gloves and was training to become a hand model. Sir Galahad had doubled in size from regular packages of Morgana's gingerbread. Sir Tristan was knitting a mega quilt made from all the enemy's captured flags. Sir Percival had raided the Camembert camp and ran off with all the runny cheese in sight. Sir Headstrong received free swimming tickets and was planning a visit to Cumbria next month.

"Nice try, Merlin," said Gawain. "But you're staying right there... until something worse comes along." (Something worse came along a year later called 'Morgana and her army of dancing skeletons'). But for the moment, Arthur had given his knights only one order to follow – keep the wizard's mischief to a minimum. Not much had happened in Camelot since the great battle and the king hoped to keep it that way. Most of the time had been spent mending things that were broken (from drawbridges to noses). Thankfully, the worst damage had been done when Sir Softpaws was a giant and he had already been forgiven for being so cute.

Just then, a man was rushing his way through the busy town square and stood on a small soap box. His arrival was the most exciting thing to have happened in Camelot for the past few weeks. This was Hark the Town Crier. He had the job of making important announcements on behalf of Arthur and Guinevere. And today he had some very, very important news.

"Hear ye! Hear ye!" yelled Hark in his most serious voice. The words boomed out loud, giving Merlin a splitting headache. Unfortunately, the wooden stocks stopped him from reaching into his pockets for a headache potion).

"Hear ye! Hear ye!" called Hark again. "I have news for all to hear." By now, the peasants had stopped what they were doing and began to listen. The Town Crier cleared his throat and gave the news.

"King Arthur has decided to take a long holiday. By order of Queen Guinevere, Sir Softpaws will be named the new Prince Regent of Camelot!"

There was a short silence before the crowd exploded into applause and cheers. Word of Sir Softpaws's rule spread through the kingdom (or cat-dom) and a big party broke up and down the cobblestone streets of Camelot. Everyone was so happy that they danced arm in arm. Food, drink and music were shared in good spirits. This was the kind of news everyone could agree was good. It began a new era of smart government and cuteness, with peace and love for human and kitty kind alike.

"A kingdom, ruled by a cat?" Merlin said with a crafty grin. "Perhaps my time has come."

A rotten tomato whizzed past the wizard's ear and splattered on the stonework behind him. His time might come later. Maybe. Possibly.

"We're the only kingdom in Britain that's ruled by a cat!" said a poor goat herder who hadn't had a meal in weeks due to the road closures that came with the battle.

"In your face§ King Fredrick of Frankia!" yelled Rudolph Shortsword. He was still easily riled up about rival kingdoms. And after the invasion and losing his dance studio, he had a point.

"Perhaps he needs a special advisor," pondered Terry Cotter, who was busy planning his next money-making move.

"Long live the cat!" cried a woman with the turnip.

"Hooray! Hurrah!" shouted the sort of people who shout things out spontaneously.

From his high tower in Camelot castle, Arthur watched the street party below. The jolly gathering went on late into the night. The only hiccup came when Sir Lid-shut fell down a well but luckily he was fished out after about 30 minutes and the party continued. Slipping on his royal dressing gown and popping on the royal slippers, Arthur made his way down the winding staircase through the castle hallway. Nobody had bothered to fix the doors to Merlin's lab, but for once, the king didn't really mind.

In the Round Table room, Guinevere was busy drawing up plans for a whole series of new defences (starting with a moat upgrade – sword-wielding sea lions and crocodile archers). She was making preparations just in case Arthur's next birthday went south. The walls of Camelot needed double thickness if the clown returned. She had also banned prunes, plums and broccoli in order to keep the kingdom safe and secure.

Arthur entered the throne room where Sir Softpaws was taking a nap. The cat was tucked up in his basket with a small bowl of cooked fish near a nice warm fireplace. It seemed he strongly preferred being an indoor cat. With a cup of tea in his hand, Arthur sat on his throne and accidentally helped himself to the cat's biscuits. It would be the fishiest cup of tea he could remember.

"Well, Sir Softpaws," began Arthur. "Now you're Prince Regent of the kingdom, what is your first royal order of business?"

But Softpaws remained sound asleep, only giving off quiet snores.

"That's exactly what I would have done," said King Arthur. "Well done that puss!"

Mogzilla presents...

The Spartapuss series - set in ancient Rome, in a world ruled by cats!

I AM SPARTAPUSS

BOOK I

Spartapuss, a ginger cat, is happy managing Rome's most famous Bath & Spa. But Fortune has other plans for him.

ISBN: 9781906132422

CATLIGULA

BOOK II

When Catligula becomes Emperor, his madness brings Rome to within a whisker of disaster.

ISBN: 9781906132484

DIE CLAWDIUS

BOOK III

The Emperor Clawdius decides to invade Spartapuss' home – The Land of the Kitons.

ISBN: 9780954657680

BOUDICAT

BOOK IV

Queen Boudicat has declared war on Rome and she wants Spartapuss to join her rebel army.

ISBN: 9781906132019

CLEOCATRA'S KUSHION

BOOK V

Spartapuss must travel through Fleagypt to the land of the Kushites and find his missing son.

ISBN: 9781906132064